Advance Praise for *Multipliers*

"*Multipliers* is a great manifesto for today's leaders. The authors provide a hands-on guide showing leaders how to make their total organization smarter by tapping the brainpower of everyone at all levels. A very timely and insightful book."

—**Noel Tichy, coauthor of *Judgment* with Warren Bennis, and Professor of Management and Organizations at the University of Michigan**

"We've all known Multipliers—people who bring the best, not the worst, out of everyone around them. They're a company's greatest resource. If you want to learn how to become a Multiplier or transform others into genuine Multipliers, read on. If you want to enhance your own career and strengthen your company, read on."

—**Kerry Patterson, bestselling author, *Crucial Conversations***

"A fascinating book that shows how mindsets shape the way people lead. This book will forever change the way we think about leadership."

—**Carol Dweck, Lewis and Virginia Eaton Professor of Psychology, Department of Psychology, Stanford University, and author of *Mindset***

"Liz Wiseman and Greg McKeown's insights are helpful, practical, and relevant. Any leader who needs to get more done with the same (or fewer) resources will find this book a gift and a valuable resource."

—**Dave Ulrich, professor, the Ross School of Business, the University of Michigan**

"This book will speak to every CEO and CFO. Multipliers get so much from their people that they effectively double their workforce for free."

—**Jeff Henley, chairman of the board, Oracle Corporation**

"*Multipliers* is a compelling read. A must-have manual for any in a leadership position or aspiring to become a leader. It's obvious Liz Wiseman and Greg McKeown did their homework, and those of us who read *Multipliers* are all the better for it." —**Byron Pitts, *60 Minutes***

"This engaging and subversive book asks a vital question: "How can we grow and harness human talent to address the great issues of our day?" *Multipliers* makes us rethink many of our old assumptions."

—**Gareth Jones, visiting professor, IE Madrid, and coauthor,**
Why Should Anyone Be Led by You?

"This book touches upon such a fundamental truth about leadership—one that has been waiting to be named, explored, and finally addressed. Liz Wiseman and Greg McKeown have created a language that will be with us for a very long time, impacting millions."

—**Verne Harnish, founder, Entrepreneurs' Organization (EO),**
and CEO, Gazelles

"*Multipliers* is brilliant and extraordinarily timely! It belongs on the bookshelf of every leader—and every leadership scholar."

—**Roderick M. Kramer, William R. Kimball Professor**
of Organizational Behavior, Stanford University School of Business

MULTIPLIERS

Multipliers

How the Best Leaders

Make Everyone Smarter

LIZ WISEMAN
WITH GREG MCKEOWN

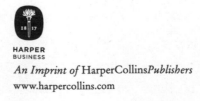

HARPER
BUSINESS
An Imprint of HarperCollins*Publishers*
www.harpercollins.com

HarperCollins books may be purchased for educational, business, or sales promotional use. For information, please write: Special Markets Department, HarperCollins Publishers, 10 East 53rd Street, New York, NY 10022.

Designed by Jaime Putorti

Library of Congress Cataloging-in-Publication Data
Wiseman, Liz.
    Multipliers : how the best leaders make everyone smarter / by Liz Wiseman with Greg McKeown.—1st ed.
        p.   cm.
    Summary: "A thought-provoking, accessible, and essential exploration of why some leaders (called 'Diminishers') drain capability and intelligence from their teams, while others (called 'Multipliers') amplify it to produce better results."
—Provided by publisher
    ISBN 978-0-06-196439-8
    1. Leadership. 2. Executive ability. 3. Employee
motivation. 4. Excellence. I. McKeown, Greg. II. Title.
HD57.7.W57   2010
658.4'092—dc22

                                                        2010002866

---

12 13 14   OV/RRD   20 19 18

To my children,
Megan, Amanda, Christian, and Joshua,
who have taught me to lead and shown me
why being a Multiplier matters.

CONTENTS

FOREWORD *by Stephen R. Covey*

I had the opportunity to work with a Multiplier when I was in my early twenties. It profoundly shaped the rest of my life. I had decided to take a break in my education to provide extended volunteer service. The invitation came to go to England. Just four and a half months after my arrival, the president of the organization came to me and said, "I have a new assignment for you. I want you to travel around the country and train local leaders." I was shocked. Who was I to train leaders in their fifties and sixties? Some of these individuals had been leading twice as long as I had been alive. Sensing my doubt, he simply looked me in the eye and said, "I have great confidence in you. You can do this. I will give you the materials to help you prepare to teach these leaders." It is hard to overstate the impact this leader had on me. By the time I returned home, I had begun to detect the work I wanted to devote my life to.

His particular ability—to get more out of people than they knew they had to give—fascinated me. I have reflected on this many times, wondering *what he did that got so much from me*. The answer to this question is contained in this book.

Liz Wiseman and her collaborator Greg McKeown have written a book that explores this idea more deeply than anything I have read elsewhere on this subject. And their timing couldn't be better.

New Demands, Insufficient Resources

At a time when many organizations do not have the luxury of adding or transferring resources to tackle major challenges, they must find the capabilities within their current ranks. The ability to extract and multiply the intelligence that already exists in the organization is red-hot relevant. Across industries and organizations of all kinds, leaders now find themselves in what David Allen has summarized as "new demands, insufficient resources."

For some forty years I have worked with organizations that were grappling with "new demands, insufficient resources." I have become convinced that the biggest leadership challenge of our times is not insufficient resources per se, but rather our inability to access the most valuable resources at our disposal.

When I ask in my seminars, "How many of you would agree that the vast majority of the workforce possesses far more capability, creativity, talent, initiative, and resourcefulness than their present jobs allow or even require them to use?" the affirmative response is about 99 percent.

Then I ask a second question: "Who here feels the pressure to produce more from less?" Again, a sea of hands goes up.

When you put those two questions together, you can see the challenge. As stated in this book, indeed, people are often "overworked and underutilized." Some corporations have made hiring the most intelligent individuals a core strategy on the basis that smarter people can solve problems more quickly than the competition. But that only works if the organizations can access that intelligence. Organizations that figure out how to better access this vastly underutilized resource won't just be more enjoyable places to work; they will outperform their competitors. In this global environment this might well make the difference between companies that make it and those that don't. And as with so many business challenges, leadership is clearly a critical force for leveraging the full capability of the organization.

The New Idea

Multipliers: How the Best Leaders Make Everyone Smarter represents nothing less than the leadership paradigm necessary for accessing the intelligence and potential of people in organizations everywhere. It unearths and explains why some leaders create genius all around them while other leaders drain intelligence and capability from an organization.

Peter Drucker spoke of what is at stake when he wrote:

> *The most important, and indeed the truly unique, contribution of management in the 20th century was the fifty-fold increase in the productivity of the manual worker in manufacturing.*
>
> *The most important contribution management needs to make in the 21st century is similarly to increase the productivity of knowledge work and the knowledge worker.*
>
> *The most valuable assets of the 20th-century company were its production equipment. The most valuable asset of a 21st-century institution, whether business or non-business, will be its knowledge workers and their productivity.[1]*

This book explains with great clarity the kinds of leaders who will answer the promise outlined by Drucker and those who will not.

As I read this book, a key insight was that Multipliers are hard-edged managers. There is nothing soft about these leaders. They expect great things from their people and drive them to achieve extraordinary results. Another insight that resonated with me was that people actually get smarter and more capable around Multipliers. That is, people don't just feel smarter; they actually become smarter. They can solve harder problems, adapt more quickly, and take more intelligent action.

People who understand these ideas will be well positioned to make the shift the authors describe from genius (where they may try to be the smartest person in the room) to genius maker (where they use their intelligence to access and multiply the genius in others). The power of such a shift is difficult to overstate. It is a night-and-day difference.

What I Love About This Book

I admire the work and insight in this book for several reasons.

First, for the journalistic integrity and sheer tenacity required to analyze over 150 executives across the Americas, Europe, Asia, and Africa. The book is full of rich and vivid examples gathered from all over the world.

Second, for the way this book focuses on just those few things that really differentiate intelligence Multipliers and intelligence Diminishers. This isn't a general book on leadership with all good qualities on one side and all bad qualities on the other. It is more precise than that, identifying and illustrating only the five most differentiated disciplines.

Third, for the book's "range of motion." This book names a phenomenon the way Malcolm Gladwell seems to be able to, but also goes down several layers to provide practical insight into exactly how to lead like a Multiplier.

Fourth, for the way the book seamlessly combines cutting-edge insight with timeless principles. Many books do one or the other. Few do both. This book will relate to your life today and it will connect to your conscience, too.

An Idea Whose Time Has Come

Liz Wiseman and Greg McKeown have written a book that is relevant for the entire world. Corporate executives will immediately see its relevance, but so will leaders in education, hospitals, foundations, nonprofit organizations, entrepreneurial start-ups, healthcare systems, middle-size businesses and government at the local, state, and national level. I believe this book is relevant to everyone from first-time managers to world leaders.

This book comes to the world at a time when it is greatly needed, a time of "new demands, insufficient resources" when CFOs and HR directors are surprisingly in synch about the need for an approach that better leverages current resources. The principles in this book will always be true, but in this economic climate they will win in the marketplace of ideas. Their relevance will give them life and attention that is deserved. These are ideas that matter *now*, and as Victor Hugo once said, "There is nothing more powerful than an idea whose time has come."

I have a vision of thousands of leaders discovering they have unintentionally diminished the people around them, and taking steps toward becoming a Multiplier. I have a vision of schools with diminishing cultures being reinvented around Multiplier principles, to the benefit of the whole community. I have a vision of world leaders learning how to better access the intelligence and capability of those they serve, to address some of the world's toughest challenges.

And so I challenge you to recognize the opportunity that is in your hands. Don't just read this book; pay the price to really become a Multiplier. Don't let this become a buzzword in your organization. Use the principles to reinvent your organization toward a true Multiplying culture that gets more out of people than they knew they had to give. Choose to be a Multiplier to people around you, as the president was to me in England all those years ago. I have great confidence in the good that can come from such an approach to leadership in your team and in your entire organization. Just imagine what would happen to our world if every leader on the planet took one step from Diminisher to Multiplier.

It can be done.

MULTIPLIERS

CHAPTER 1

THE MULTIPLIER EFFECT

It has been said that after meeting with the great
British Prime Minister William Ewart Gladstone, you
left feeling he was the smartest person in the world,
but after meeting with his rival Benjamin Disraeli, you
left thinking you were the smartest person.[1]

BONO

During the summer of 1987 Gabriel Oz, like virtually all of his peers, entered the army as part of the national military obligation of Israeli citizens to serve in a combat unit. Gabriel, a smart, confident eighteen-year-old with a boisterous laugh, was selected for tank commander instruction and sent to the Golan Heights for basic training.

After six months of training, Gabriel and six of his peers were selected out of basic training for special assignment. There was an urgent need for soldiers to patrol the six-mile-deep belt along the border between Lebanon and Israel. In lieu of completing the remaining three months of basic training, these young soldiers were deployed to Lebanon and would soon experience real combat conditions. Gabriel and his peers faced a complex and chaotic set of battle conditions as they woke the next day in the field to the sound of gunfire and bombs. Under these intense circumstances, Gabriel worked well with his commanders and was considered a star for his intelligence and his ability to surmise situations quickly and accurately.

After three months of real-world experience, with ten times the amount of in-tank hours that their peers had received at basic training, Gabriel and his fellow soldiers returned to their class in the south of Israel just as the class completed basic training. As they entered the more advanced tank commander training, they experienced a change of command and were assigned to serve under a new commanding officer, Yuval.[2]

Yuval was considered to be the cream of the crop—the top 0.1 percent of talent—and had been fast-tracked through basic training after having left the elite pilot training program due to a medical issue. He was an intelligent and highly skilled tank commander who had just received officer status. But it appeared he still had a reputation to build and something to prove—to Gabriel in particular.

Yuval had a superior knowledge of tank operations and flaunted it as if competing with Gabriel's battlefield savvy. During navigational exercises, Yuval publicly mocked Gabriel and his team's efforts when they failed to find all the designated waypoints. As the scrutiny of their performance continued, Gabriel and his team became less and less capable. Within a week, Gabriel was convinced he couldn't navigate.

In a typical tank maneuver, the tank commander must observe the terrain, find the enemy, command the gunner, aim, shoot, and hit the target—all in rapid succession and while being fired upon by the enemy. Hundreds of things are happening at once that need to be processed, prioritized, decided, and acted upon. Successful completion of these drills requires intense concentration and keen mental aptitude. These maneuvers are particularly intimidating because the commanding officer sits ten inches above the tank commander's head, in a special chair bolted on top of the tank. Commanding officers watch every decision and take constant notes on clipboards attached to their thighs. Gabriel now performed these maneuvers under the wary inspection of Yuval.

In the training field, Gabriel didn't just perform poorly in one maneuver; he nearly failed every maneuver. He was stellar in the classroom, but every time he took command of the tank while Yuval was mounted in the chair, he failed. As Yuval barked orders, controlled every detail, and found every mistake, the tension mounted. Gabriel got tense, couldn't think properly, and struggled to perform.

The failure was so clear that Yuval recommended to the dismissal committee that Gabriel be ejected from the tank commander program. Protocol for dismissal required that Gabriel perform a maneuver under the supervision of the company commander, Lior, the highest-ranking officer in the program. Gabriel considered his fate if he failed officer training and returned to the battlefield with just the rank of a soldier. Gabriel's friends wished him luck in this, the most stressful of situations.

The company commander took Gabriel out for his dismissal test, which consisted of a single maneuver, the Ringo—the most complex maneuver in the test suite. In the Ringo, nothing is scripted and conditions change constantly and unpredictably. Prior to entering the tank, the company commander stopped Gabriel at a model of the battlegrounds. Lior pointed out various aspects of the terrain and said, "Gabriel, what are we going to do here?" And "If the enemy moves here, how will you respond?" Lior was calm and inquisitive. Gabriel no longer felt like he was being tested. He felt like he was learning and working together with Lior to solve a challenge. With Lior now in the chair above him, Gabriel performed the most complex maneuver beautifully—perfectly, even. As Gabriel completed the drill, Lior dismounted from the chair and said, "You are not dismissed."

Gabriel continued with his tank commander training, performing the maneuvers under a different sergeant, all with stellar results. Lior placed Gabriel in the top 10 percent of the class and nominated him to go directly to the officer academy, where he again faced difficult navigational exercises. Interestingly, he found all the waypoints and consistently returned in the top of his class. Curiously, he had become a great navigator once again.

Gabriel completed officer training and was asked to become a *ganan*, Hebrew for a commanding officer who trains or cultivates other officers. He finished his time in the Israeli army as a major and then went on to a successful career in technology, both in Israel and the United States where, incidentally, he found his performance again rising and falling under leaders much like Yuval and Lior.

Gabriel's army experience illustrates that often a change in command can cause a change in capability. Gabriel was smart and capable under one leader, but stupefied with fear under another. What did Yuval say and do that so diminished Gabriel's intelligence and capability? And what did Lior do that restored and expanded Gabriel's ability to reason and navigate complexity?

Some leaders make us better and smarter. They bring out our intelligence. This book is about these leaders, who access and revitalize the intelligence in the people around them. We call them Multipliers. This book will show you why they create genius around them and make everyone smarter and more capable.

QUESTIONING GENIUS

There are bird watchers, and there are whale watchers. I'm a genius watcher. I am fascinated by the intelligence of others. I notice it, study it, and have learned to identify a variety of types of intelligence. Oracle Corporation, the $22 billion software giant, was a great place for genius watching. In the seventeen years I worked in senior management at Oracle, I was fortunate to work alongside many intelligent executives, all systematically recruited from the best companies and out of elite universities as top performers. Because I worked as the vice president responsible for the company's global talent development strategy and ran the corporate university, I worked closely with these executives and had a front-row seat to study their leadership. From this vantage point, I began to observe how they used their intelligence in very different ways, and I became intrigued by the effect they had on the people in their organizations.

The Problem with Genius

Some leaders seemed to drain intelligence and capability out of the people around them. Their focus on their own intelligence and their resolve to be the smartest person in the room had a diminishing effect on everyone else. For them to look smart, other people had to end up looking dumb. We've all worked with these black holes. They create a vortex that sucks energy out of everyone and everything around them. When they walk into a room, the shared IQ drops and the length of the meeting doubles. In countless settings, these leaders were idea killers and energy destroyers. Other people's ideas suffocated and died in their presence and the flow of intelligence came to an abrupt halt around them. Around these leaders, intelligence flowed only one way: from them to others.

Other leaders used their intelligence in a fundamentally different way. They applied their intelligence to amplify the smarts and capability of people around them. People got smarter and better in their presence. Ideas grew; challenges were surmounted; hard problems were solved. When these leaders walked into a room, light bulbs started going off over people's heads. Ideas flew so fast that you had to replay the meeting in slow motion just to see what was going on. Meetings with them were idea mash-up sessions. These leaders seemed to make everyone around them better and more capable. These leaders weren't just intelligent themselves—they were intelligence Multipliers.

Perhaps these leaders understood that the person sitting at the apex of the intelligence hierarchy is the genius maker, not the genius.

Post-Oracle Therapy

The idea for this book emerged from my post-Oracle therapy. Leaving Oracle was like stepping off a high-speed bullet train and suddenly finding everything moving in slow motion. This sudden calm gave way to wonder about the lingering question: How do some leaders create intelligence around them, while others diminish it?

As I began teaching and coaching executives, I saw the same dynamic playing out in other companies. Some leaders seemed to boost the collective IQ while others sucked the mental life out of their employees. I found myself working with highly intelligent executives who were struggling with their own tendency to either overtly or subtly shut down the people around them. I also worked with many senior leaders struggling to make better use of their resources. Most of these leaders had developed their leadership skills during times of growth. However, in a more austere business climate, they found themselves unable to solve problems by simply throwing more resources at the problem. They needed to find ways to boost the productivity of the people they already had.

I recall one particularly pivotal conversation with a client named Dennis Moore, a senior executive with a genius-level IQ. As we discussed how leaders can have an infectious effect on the intelligence in their organization and spark viral intelligence, he responded, "These leaders are like amplifiers. They are intelligence amplifiers."

Yes, certain leaders amplify intelligence. These leaders, whom we have come to call Multipliers, create collective, viral intelligence in organizations. Other leaders act as Diminishers and deplete the organization of crucial intelligence and capability. But what is it that these Multipliers do? What is it that Multipliers do differently than Diminishers?

Scouring business school journals and the Internet looking for answers to these questions, as well as for resources for clients, yielded only frustration. This void set the course for my research into this phenomenon. I was determined to find answers for leaders wanting to multiply the intelligence of their organizations.

The Research

The first major discovery was finding the perfect research partner, Greg McKeown, who was studying at Stanford University's Graduate School of Business. Greg, originally from London, England, had worked as both a management advisor and a leadership development analyst for global companies. Greg has a curious and tenacious mind and a passion for leadership that gave him my same measure of determination to find the answers. After I convinced Greg to divert from a PhD program, we formalized our research effort and went to work. Greg brought rigor to our analysis and our debates and asked the hard questions as we wrote up our findings. He has focused on teaching and testing these ideas inside organizations, which has allowed me to teach and write, giving voice to the ideas I have observed and studied for many years.

We began our formal research by defining the question that would consume us for the next two years: "What are the vital few differences between intelligence Diminishers and intelligence Multipliers, and what impact do they have on organizations?" Waking up for 730 days with the same question was like the movie *Groundhog Day*, in which Bill Murray wakes each day to the same time and song on his alarm clock, destined to repeat the events of the previous day. In the singular and prolonged pursuit of this question, Greg and I began to develop a deep understanding of this Multiplier effect.

We began our research by selecting a set of companies and industries in which individual and organizational intelligence provide a competitive advantage. Because these organizations rise or fall based on the strength of their intellectual assets, we assumed the Multiplier effect would be pronounced. We interviewed senior professionals inside these organizations, asking them to identify two leaders, one who fit the description of a Multiplier and one a Diminisher. We studied more than 150 of the resulting leaders through interviews and a quantitative assessment of their leadership practices. For many leaders, we then followed an intensive 360 degree interview process with both former and current members of their management teams.

As our research expanded, we studied additional leaders from other companies and industries, looking for common elements that spanned the business and nonprofit sectors as well as geographies. Our research journey took us across four continents and introduced us to an incredibly rich and diverse set of leaders. We came to know some of these leaders quite well, studying them and their organizations in depth.

Two of the leaders we studied provided a sharp contrast between these two leadership styles. They both worked for the same company and in the same role. One had the Midas touch of a Multiplier and the other had the chilling effect of a Diminisher.

A TALE OF TWO MANAGERS

Vikram[3] worked as an engineering manager under two different division managers at Intel. Each leader could be considered a genius. Both had a profound impact on Vikram. The first leader was George Schneer, who was a division manager for one of Intel's businesses.

Manager #1: The Midas Touch

George had a reputation for running successful businesses at Intel. Every business he ran was profitable and grew under his leadership. But what most distinguished George was the impact he had on the people around him.

Vikram said, "I was a rock star around George. He *made* me. Because of him I transitioned from an individual contributor to big-time manager. Around him, I felt like a smart SOB—everyone felt like that. He got 100 percent from me—it was exhilarating." George's team echoed the same sentiments: "We are not sure exactly what George did, but we knew we were smart and we were winning. Being on this team was the highlight of our careers."

George grew people's intelligence by engaging it. He wasn't the center of attention and didn't worry about how smart he looked. What George worried about was extracting the smarts and maximum effort from each member of his team. In a typical meeting, he spoke only about 10 percent of the time, mostly just to "crisp up" the problem statement. He would then back away and give his team space to figure out an answer. Often the ideas his team would generate were worth millions. George's team drove the business to achieve outstanding revenue growth and to deliver the profit bridge that allowed Intel to enter the microprocessor business.

Manager #2: The Idea Killer

Several years later, Vikram moved out of George's group and went to work for a second division manager who had been the architect of one of the early microprocessors. This second manager was a brilliant scientist who had now been promoted into management to run the plant that produced the chips. He was highly intelligent by every measure and left his mark on everyone and everything around him.

The problem was that this leader did all the thinking. Vikram said, "He was very, very smart. But people had a way of shutting down around him. He just killed our ideas. In a typical team meeting, he did about 30 percent of the talking and left little space for others. He gave a lot of feedback—most of it was about how bad our ideas were."

This manager made all the decisions himself or with a single confidant. He would then announce those decisions to the organization. Vikram said, "You always knew he would have an answer for everything. He had really strong opinions and put his energy into selling his ideas to others and convincing them to execute on the details. No one else's opinion mattered."

This manager hired intelligent people, but they soon realized that they didn't have permission to think for themselves. Eventually, they would quit or threaten to quit. Ultimately Intel hired a second-in-command to work alongside this manager to counter the intelligence drain on the organization. But even then, Vikram said, "My job was more like cranking than creating. He really only got from me about 50 percent of what I had to offer. And I would *never* work for him again!"

Diminisher or Multiplier?

The second leader was so absorbed in his own intelligence that he stifled others and diluted the organization's crucial intelligence and capability. George brought out the intelligence in others and created collective, viral intelligence in his organization. One leader was a genius. The other was a genius maker.

It isn't how much you know that matters. What matters is how much access you have to what other people know. It isn't just how intelligent your team members are; it is how much of that intelligence you can draw out and put to use.

We've all experienced these two types of leaders. What type of leader are you right now? Are you a genius, or are you a genius maker?

THE MULTIPLIER EFFECT

Multipliers are genius makers. Everyone around them gets smarter and more capable. People may not become geniuses in a traditional sense, but Multipliers invoke each person's unique intelligence and create an atmosphere of genius—innovation, productive effort, and collective intelligence.

In studying Multipliers and Diminishers, we learned that at the most fundamental level, they get dramatically different results from their people, they hold a different logic and set of assumptions about people's intelligence, and they do a small number of things very differently. Let's first examine the impact of the Multipliers—why people get smarter and more capable around them and why they get twice as much from their resources as do the Diminishers. We call this the Multiplier effect.

Because Multipliers are leaders who look beyond their own genius and focus their energy on extracting and extending the genius of others, they get more from their people. They don't get a little more; they get vastly more.

2X Multiplier Effect

The impact of a Multiplier can be seen in two ways: first, from the point of view of the people they work with and second, from the point of view of the organizations they shape and create. Let's begin by examining how Multipliers influence the people who work around them.

Extracting Intelligence

Multipliers extract all of the capability from people. In our interviews, people told us that Multipliers got *a lot* more out of them than Diminishers. We asked each person to identify the percentage of their capability that a Diminisher received from them. The numbers typically ranged between 20 and 50 percent. When we asked them to identify the percentage of their capability that the Multiplier extracted, the numbers typically fell between 70 and 100 percent.[4] When we compared the two sets of data, we were amazed to find that Multipliers got 1.97 times more. That represents an almost twofold increase or a 2X effect. After concluding our formal research, we continued to pose this question in workshops and with management teams, asking people to reflect on their past Multiplier and Diminisher bosses. Across industries and in the public, private, and nonprofit sectors, we continued to find that Multipliers get at least two times more from people.

What could you accomplish if you could get twice as much from your people?

The reason for the difference is that when people work with Multipliers, they hold nothing back. They offer the very best of their thinking, creativity, and ideas. They give more than their jobs require and volunteer their discretionary effort, energy, and resourcefulness. They actively search for more valuable ways to contribute. They hold themselves to the highest standards. They give 100 percent of their abilities to the work—and then some.

Extending Intelligence

Not only do Multipliers extract capability and intelligence from people, they do it in a way that extends and grows that intelligence. In our interviews people often said Multipliers accessed *more* than 100 percent of their capability. They would say, "Oh, they got 120 percent from me." Initially, I pushed back, citing that getting more than 100 percent is mathematically impossible. But we continued to hear people claim Multipliers got more than 100 percent from them. Greg pushed this issue, suggesting this pattern was an important data point. We began to ask: Why would people insist that intelligence Multipliers got more out of them than they actually had?

Our research confirmed that Multipliers not only access people's current capability, they stretch it. They get more from people than they knew they had to give. People reported actually getting smarter around Multipliers. The implication is that intelligence itself can grow.

This is an insight that is corroborated by other recent research into the extensible nature of intelligence. Consider a few recent studies:

- Carol Dweck of Stanford University has conducted groundbreaking research that found that children given a series of progressively harder puzzles and praised for their intelligence stagnate for fear of reaching the limit of their intelligence. Children given the same series of puzzles but then praised for their hard work actually increased their ability to reason and to solve problems. When these children were recognized for their efforts to think, they created a belief, and then a reality, that intelligence grows.[5]

■ Eric Turkheimer of the University of Virginia has found that bad environments suppress children's IQs. When poor children were adopted into upper-middle-class households, their IQs rose by 12 to 18 points.[6]

■ Richard Nisbett of the University of Michigan has reviewed studies that show: 1) students' IQ levels drop over summer vacation, and 2) IQ levels across society have steadily increased over time. The average IQ of people in 1917 would amount to a mere 73 on today's IQ test.[7]

After reading these studies, I took Greg's advice and recalculated the data from our research interviews at face value, using the literal percentage of capability that people claimed Multipliers received from them. When factoring this excess capability (the amount beyond 100 percent) into our calculations, we found that Multipliers actually get 2.1 times more than Diminishers. What if you not only got 2X more from your team—what if you could get everything they had to give plus a 5 to 10 percent growth bonus because they were getting smarter and more capable while working for you?

This 2X effect is a result of the deep leverage Multipliers get from their resources. When you extrapolate the 2X Multiplier effect to the organization, you begin to see the strategic relevance. Simply said, resource leverage creates competitive advantage.

Resource Leverage

When Tim Cook, COO of Apple Inc., opened a budget review in one sales division, he reminded the management team that the strategic imperative was revenue growth. Everyone expected this but they were astounded when he asked for the growth *without* providing additional headcount. The sales executive at the meeting said he thought the revenue target was attainable but only *with* more headcount. He suggested they follow a proven linear model of incremental headcount growth, insisting that everyone knows that more revenue means you need more headcount. The two executives continued the conversation for months, never fully able to bridge their logic. The sales executive was speaking the language of addition (that is, higher growth by adding more resources). The COO was speaking the language of multiplication (that is, higher growth by better utilizing the resources that already exist).

The Logic of Addition

This is the dominant logic that has existed in corporate planning: that resources will be added when new requests are made. Senior executives ask for more output and the next layer of operational leaders request more headcount. The negotiations go back and forth until everyone settles on a scenario such as: 20 percent more output with 5 percent more resources. Neither the senior executive nor the operational leaders are satisfied.

Operational leaders entrenched in the logic of resource allocation and addition argue:

1. Our people are overworked.

2. Our best people are the most maxed out.

3. Therefore, accomplishing a bigger task requires the addition of more resources.

This is the logic of addition. It seems persuasive but, importantly, it ignores the opportunity to more deeply leverage existing resources. The logic of addition creates a scenario in which people become both overworked *and* underutilized. To argue for allocation without giving attention to resource leverage is an expensive corporate norm.

Business school professors and strategy gurus Gary Hamel and C.K. Prahalad have written, "The resource allocation task of top management has received too much attention when compared to the task of resource leverage. . . . If top management devotes more effort to assessing the strategic feasibility of projects in its allocation role than it does to the task of multiplying resource effectiveness, its value-added will be modest indeed."[8]

Picture a child at a buffet line. They load up on food, but a lot of it is left on the plate uneaten. The food gets picked at and pushed around, but it is left to go to waste. Like these children, Diminishers are eager to load up on resources, and they might even get the job done, but many people are left unused; their capability wasted. Consider the costs of one high-flying product development executive at a technology firm.

THE HIGH-COST DIMINISHER Jasper Wallis[9] talked a good game. He was smart and could articulate a compelling vision for his products and their transformational benefits for customers. Jasper was also politically savvy and knew how to play politics. The problem was that Jasper's organization could not execute and realize the promise of his vision because they were in a perpetual spin cycle, spinning around him.

Jasper was a strategist and an idea man. However, his brain worked faster and produced more ideas than his organization could execute. Every week or so, he would launch a new focus or a new initiative. His director of operations recalled, "He'd tell us on Monday, we needed to catch up with 'competitor X,' and we needed to get it done this week." The organization would scurry, throw a "Hail Mary" pass, and make progress for a few days, and then eventually lose traction when they were given a new goal to chase the following week.

This leader was so heavily involved in the details that he became a bottleneck in the organization. He worked extremely hard, but his organization moved slowly. His need to micromanage limited what the rest of the organization could contribute. His need to put his personal stamp on everything wasted resources and meant his division of 1,000 was only operating at about 500 strong.

Jasper's modus operandi was to compete for resources with a larger division in the company that produced similar technology. Jasper's overriding goal was to outsize the other division. He hired people at a breakneck pace and built his own internal infrastructure and staff—all of which was redundant with infrastructure that existed in the other division. He even convinced the company to build a dedicated office tower for his division.

Things eventually caught up with Jasper. It became clear that his products were hype and the company was losing market share. When the real return on investment (ROI) calculation was made, he was removed from the company and his division was folded into the other product group. The duplicate infrastructure he built was eventually removed, but only after many millions of dollars had been wasted and opportunities lost in the market.

Diminishers come at a high cost.

The Logic of Multiplication

We have examined the logic of addition and the resource inefficiencies that follow. Better leverage and utilization of resources at the organizational level require adopting a new corporate logic. This new logic is one of multiplication. Instead of achieving linear growth by adding new resources, you can more efficiently extract the capability of your people and watch growth skyrocket.

Leaders rooted in the logic of multiplication believe:

1. Most people in organizations are underutilized.

2. All capability can be leveraged with the right kind of leadership.

3. Therefore, intelligence and capability can be multiplied without requiring a bigger investment.

For example, when Apple Inc. needed to achieve rapid growth with flat resources in one division, they didn't expand their sales force. Instead, they gathered the key players across the various job functions, took a week to study the problem, and collaboratively developed a solution. They changed the sales model to utilize competency centers and better leverage their best salespeople and deep industry experts in the sales cycle. They achieved year-over-year growth in the double digits with virtually flat resources.

Salesforce.com, a $1 billion software firm that has pioneered software as a service, has been making the shift from the logic of addition to the logic of multiplication. They enjoyed a decade of outstanding growth using the old idea of "throwing resources at a problem." They addressed new customers and new demands by hiring the best technical and business talent available and deploying them on the challenges. However, a strained market environment created a new imperative for the company's leadership: get more productivity from their currently available resources. They could no longer operate on outdated notions of resource utilization. They started developing leaders who could multiply the intelligence and capability of the people around them and increase the brainpower of the organization to meet their growth demands.

Resource leverage is a far richer concept than just "accomplish more with less." Multipliers don't necessarily get more with less. They get more by using more—more of people's intelligence and capability. As one CEO put it, "Eighty people can either operate with the productivity of fifty or they can operate as though they were five hundred." And because these Multipliers achieve better resource efficiency, they enjoy a strengthened competitive position against companies entrenched in the logic of addition.

This book strikes at the root of this outdated logic. To begin to see how, we will turn to the question of how Multipliers access intelligence and get so much from people. The answer, we found, is in the mindset and the five disciplines of the Multiplier.

THE MIND OF THE MULTIPLIER

As we studied both Diminishers and Multipliers, we consistently found that they hold radically different assumptions about the intelligence of the people they work with. These assumptions appear to explain much of the difference in how Diminishers and Multipliers operate.

THE MIND OF THE DIMINISHER The Diminisher's view of intelligence is based on elitism and scarcity. Diminishers appear to believe that *really intelligent people are a rare breed* and *I am one of the few really smart people.* They then conclude, *other people will never figure things out without me.*

I recall a leader I worked with whom I can only describe as an "intellectual supremacist." This senior executive ran a technology organization of over 4,000 highly educated knowledge workers. Most of these employees were graduates of top universities from around the world. I joined one of his management meetings in which twenty members of his senior management team were troubleshooting an important go-to-market problem for one of their products. As we walked out of the meeting, we were reflecting on the conversation and the decisions made. He stopped, turned to me, and calmly said, "In meetings, I typically only listen to a couple of people. No one else really has anything to offer." I think he saw the alarm on my face because after his words came out, he added the awkward postscript, "Well, of course you are one of these people." I doubted it. Out of the top twenty managers representing a division of 4,000 people, he believed only a couple had anything to offer. As we walked down the hallway, we passed by rows and rows of cubicles and offices occupied by his staff. Seen through new eyes, this expanse now suddenly looked like a massive brainpower wasteland. I wanted to make a public announcement and tell them all that they could go home since their senior executive didn't think they had much to offer.

In addition to assuming intelligence is a scarce commodity, Diminishers see intelligence as static, meaning it doesn't change over time or circumstance. Our research showed that Diminishers see intelligence as something basic about a person that can't change much. This is consistent with what Dr. Carol Dweck, noted psychologist and author, calls a "fixed mindset," which is a belief that one's intelligence and qualities are carved in stone.[10] Diminishers' two-step logic appears to be *people who don't "get it" now, never will*; therefore, *I'll need to keep doing the thinking for everyone*. In the Diminisher world, there is no vacation for the smart people!

You can probably predict how the executive described above actually operated on a day-to-day basis. You might ask yourself how *you* would operate if, deep down, you held these beliefs. You would probably tell people what to do, make all the important decisions, and jump in and take over when someone appeared to be failing. And in the end, you would almost always be right, because your assumptions would cause you to manage in a way that produced subordination and dependency.

THE MIND OF THE MULTIPLIER Multipliers hold very different assumptions. Multipliers have a rich view of the intelligence of the people around them. If Diminishers see the world of intelligence in black and white, Multipliers see it in Technicolor. They don't see a world where just a few people deserve to do the thinking; Multipliers see intelligence as continually developing. This observation is consistent with what Dweck calls a "growth mindset," which is a belief that basic qualities like intelligence and ability can be cultivated through effort.[11] They assume: *people are smart and will figure it out*. They see their organization as full of talented people who are capable of contributing at much higher levels. They think like one manager we interviewed who takes stock of her team members by asking herself, *In what way is this* *person smart?* In answering this question, she finds colorful capabilities often hidden just below the surface. Instead of writing people off as not worth her time, she is able to ask, What could be done to develop and grow these capabilities? She then finds an assignment that both stretches the individual and furthers the interests of the organization.

Such Multipliers look at the complex opportunities and challenges swirling around them and assume: *there are smart people everywhere who will figure this out and get even smarter in the process.* Therefore, they conclude that their job is to bring the right people together in an environment that liberates people's best thinking and then to get out of their way.

How would you operate if you held these assumptions? In the most trying times, you would trust your people; you would extend hard challenges to them and allow them space to fulfill their responsibilities. You would access their intelligence in a way that would actually make them smarter.

The chart below summarizes how these very different sets of assumptions have a powerful effect on the way Diminishers and Multipliers lead others:

How would you:	Diminisher "They will never figure this out without me."	Multiplier "People are smart and will figure this out."
Manage talent?	Use	Develop
Approach mistakes?	Blame	Explore
Set direction?	Tell	Challenge
Make decisions?	Decide	Consult
Get things done?	Control	Support

These core assumptions are essential to unearth and understand because, quite simply, behavior follows assumptions. If someone wants to lead like a Multiplier, he or she can't simply mimic the practices of the Multiplier. An aspiring Multiplier must start by thinking like a Multiplier. In twenty years of watching and coaching executives,

I have observed how leaders' assumptions affect their management. When someone begins by examining and potentially upgrading their core assumptions, they will more easily adopt the five disciplines of the Multiplier with authenticity and impact.

THE FIVE DISCIPLINES OF THE MULTIPLIER

So what are the practices that distinguish the Multiplier? In analyzing data on over 150 leaders, we found a number of areas in which Multipliers and Diminishers do the same thing. They both are customer driven. Both have strong business acumen and market insight. Both surround themselves with smart people, and both consider themselves thought leaders. However, as we searched the data for the active ingredients unique to Multipliers, we found five disciplines in which Multipliers differentiate themselves from Diminishers.

1. ATTRACT AND OPTIMIZE TALENT. Multipliers lead people by operating as *Talent Magnets*, whereby they attract and deploy talent to its fullest regardless of who owns the resource. People flock to work with them directly or otherwise because they know they will grow and be successful. In contrast, Diminishers operate as *Empire Builders*, insisting that they must own and control resources to be more productive. They tend to divide resources into those they own and those they don't, allowing these artificial separations to hamstring effective use of all resources. People may initially be attracted to work with a Diminisher, but it is often the place where people's careers die.

The Diminisher is an Empire Builder. The Multiplier is a Talent Magnet.

2. CREATE INTENSITY THAT REQUIRES BEST THINKING. Multipliers establish a unique and highly motivating work environment where everyone has permission to think and the space to do their best work. Multipliers operate as *Liberators*, producing a climate that is both comfortable *and* intense. They remove fear and create the safety that invites people to do their best thinking. But they also create an intense environment that demands people's best effort. In contrast, Diminishers operate as *Tyrants*, introducing a fear of judgment that has a chilling effect on people's thinking and work. They demand people's best thinking, yet they don't get it.

The Diminisher is a Tyrant. The Multiplier is a Liberator.

3. EXTEND CHALLENGES. Multipliers operate as *Challengers* by seeding opportunities, laying down a challenge that stretches an organization, and generating belief that it can be done. In this way, they challenge themselves and others to push beyond what they know. In contrast, Diminishers operate as *Know-It-Alls*, personally giving directives to showcase their knowledge. While Diminishers set direction, Multipliers ensure direction gets set.

The Diminisher is a Know-It-All. The Multiplier is a Challenger.

4. DEBATE DECISIONS. Multipliers make decisions in a way that readies the organization to execute those decisions. They operate as *Debate Makers*, driving sound decisions through rigorous debate. They engage people in debating the issues up front, which leads to decisions that people understand and can execute efficiently. In contrast, Diminishers operate as *Decision Makers* who tend to make decisions efficiently within a small inner circle, but they leave the broader organization in the dark to debate the soundness of the decision instead of executing it.

The Diminisher is a Decision Maker. The Multiplier is a Debate Maker.

5. INSTILL OWNERSHIP AND ACCOUNTABILITY. Multipliers deliver and sustain superior results by inculcating high expectations across the organization. By serving as *Investors*, Multipliers provide necessary resources for success. In addition, they hold people accountable for their commitments. Over time, Multipliers' high expectations turn into an unrelenting presence, driving people to hold themselves and each other accountable, often to higher standards and without the direct intervention of the Multiplier. In contrast, Diminishers serve as *Micromanagers* who drive results by holding on to ownership, jumping into the details, and directly managing for results.

The Diminisher is a Micromanager. The Multiplier is an Investor.

The following chart summarizes the five vital disciplines that differentiate Diminishers and Multipliers:

THE 5 DISCIPLINES OF THE MULTIPLIERS

Diminisher		Multiplier	
The Empire Builder	Hoards resources and underutilizes talent	The Talent Magnet	Attracts talented people and uses them at their highest point of contribution
The Tyrant	Creates a tense environment that suppresses people's thinking and capability	The Liberator	Creates an intense environment that requires people's best thinking and work
The Know-It-All	Gives directives that showcase how much they know	The Challenger	Defines an opportunity that causes people to stretch
The Decision Maker	Makes centralized, abrupt decisions that confuse the organization	The Debate Maker	Drives sound decisions through rigorous debate
The Micro Manager	Drives results through their personal involvement	The Investor	Gives other people the ownership for results and invests in their success

SURPRISING FINDINGS

As we studied Multipliers across the world, we found a remarkable amount of consistency and several patterns that confirmed our early observations. But here are three findings that were surprising and intriguing.

A Hard Edge

One of the most critical insights from our study of Multipliers is how hard edged these managers are. They expect great things from their people and they drive people to achieve extraordinary results. They are beyond results-driven managers. They are tough and exacting. Indeed, Multipliers make people feel smart and capable; but Multipliers aren't "feel-good" managers. They look into people and find capability, and they want to access all of it. They utilize people to their fullest. They see a lot, so they expect a lot.

During our research interviews, people oozed appreciation for the Multipliers they had worked with, but the gratitude was rooted in the deep satisfaction found in working with them, not in the pleasantries of a relationship. One person described working with Deb Lange, a senior vice president of taxation at a large firm: "Working with her was like an intense workout. It was exhausting but totally exhilarating." Another said of his manager: "He got things from me I didn't know I had to give. I would do almost anything to not disappoint him."

The Multiplier approach to management isn't just an enlightened view of leadership. It is an approach that delivers higher performance because it gets vastly more out of people and returns to them a richly satisfying experience. As one early reader of this book noted, these leaders aren't about "cupcakes and kisses."

A Great Sense of Humor

It turns out that Multipliers have a great sense of humor. On a whim we added "Great Sense of Humor" to our leadership survey. Our suspicion proved right. Not only is this trait prominent among Multipliers, it is one of the traits that is most negatively correlated with the mindset held by Diminishers. Multipliers aren't necessarily comedians, but they don't take themselves or situations too seriously. Perhaps because they don't need to defend their own intelligence, Multipliers can laugh at themselves and see comedy in error and in life's foibles. Their sense of humor liberates others.

The humor of the Multiplier is very George Clooney–esque— a self-depreciating wit and an ability to put others at ease, allowing people to be themselves. As one journalist wrote of Clooney, "After fifteen minutes, he made me feel comfortable in my own house."[12] A Clooney costar said, "He has a way of daring you . . . which can be irresistible." Multipliers use humor to create comfort and to spark a natural energy and intelligence in others.

The Accidental Diminisher

Perhaps one of our biggest surprises was realizing how few Diminishers understood the restrictive impact they were having on others. Most of the Diminishers had grown up praised for their personal intelligence and had moved up the management ranks on account of personal—and often intellectual—merit. When they became "the boss," they assumed it was their job to be the smartest and to manage a set of "subordinates." Others had once had the mind and even the heart of the Multiplier, but they had been working among Diminishers for so long that they inherited many of their practices and absorbed their worldview. As one executive put it, "When I read your findings, I realized that I have been living in Diminisher land so long that I have gone native." Many people have worked for Diminishers and, although they may have escaped unscathed, they carry some of the residual effects in their own leadership. The good news for the Accidental Diminisher is that there is a viable path to becoming a Multiplier.

THE PROMISE OF THIS BOOK

As we studied Multipliers and Diminishers, we heard case after case of smart individuals being underutilized by their leaders. We heard their frustration as they told us how little some leaders got from them, despite how hard they were working and how they tried to give more. We learned that it is indeed possible to be both overworked and underutilized. Latent talent exists everywhere. Organizations are replete with underchallenged masses.

Multipliers are out there. Multipliers know how to find this dormant intelligence, challenge it, and put it to use at its fullest. They exist in business, in education, in nonprofits, and in government. Consider just a few that you will learn more about later.

1. Narayana Murthy, founder and chairman of India-based Infosys Technologies, who led the company over a twenty-year period, growing revenue to $4.6 billion and becoming one of India's largest and most successful companies (with over 100,000 professionals) by hiring people smarter than himself, giving them room to contribute, and building a management team that would succeed him without skipping a beat.

2. Sue Siegel, former biotech president turned venture capitalist for Mohr Davidow Ventures (MDV), whose partner says, "There is a Sue effect. Everything around her gets better and companies grow under her guidance. I often wonder what people are like when they aren't around Sue."

3. Lutz Ziob, general manager of Microsoft Learning, whose team says of him, "He creates an environment where good things happen. He recruits great people, allows them to make mistakes, and ferociously debates the important decisions. He demands our best, but then shares the success with the whole team."

4. Larry Gelwix, head coach of Highland Rugby, whose high school varsity team's record is 392 wins and just nine losses in thirty-four years. He attributes this extraordinary record to a deliberate leadership philosophy that engages the intelligence of his players on and off the field.

5. K.R. Sridhar, successful green-tech entrepreneur and CEO, who recruits $A+$ talent, then gives them an environment with a lot of pressure but very little stress, and allows them to experiment and take risks until the right technology and solutions emerge.

Leaders like these provide an aspiration point for those who would be Multipliers.

The promise of this book is simple: You can be a Multiplier. You can create genius around you and receive a higher contribution from your people. You can choose to think like a Multiplier and operate like one. This book will show you how. And it will show you why it matters.

This is a book for every manager trying to navigate the resource strain of tough economic times. It is a message for leaders who must accomplish more by getting more out of their people. As companies shed excess resources, the need for leaders who can multiply the intelligence and capability around them is more vital than ever. This book is also for the raging Multiplier who seeks to better understand what he or she does naturally. It is for the aspiring Multiplier who wishes to get the full capability and intelligence from his or her people. And it is most certainly for the Diminishers, so they can better understand the negative effects of leadership centered on their own intelligence. It is for every manager seeking the promise of the Multiplier: to increase intelligence everywhere and with everyone.

As you read this book, you will find a few central messages:

1. Diminishers underutilize people and leave capability on the table.

2. Multipliers increase intelligence in people and in organizations. People actually get smarter and more capable around them.

3. Multipliers leverage their resources. Corporations can get 2X more from their resources by turning their most intelligent resources into intelligence Multipliers.

Before turning our attention to the practices of the Multiplier, let's clarify what this book is not. This book is not a prescription for a nice-guy, feel-good model of leadership. It is a hard-edged approach to management that allows people to contribute more of their abilities. And although there will be much discussion of Multipliers and Diminishers, this book isn't about what they achieve themselves. It is about the impact that these leaders have on others. It is about the impact and the promise of the Multiplier. And lastly, the ideas offered in this book are not intended to be terms for labeling your diminishing boss and your colleagues. Rather, it is offered as a framework for helping you to develop the practices of a Multiplier.

This book has been designed as an end-to-end learning experience, offering an opportunity to both understand and implement the Multiplier ideas. This introduction has provided a first glance into the Multiplier effect and an overview of what Multipliers do. The successive chapters will clarify the differences between Multipliers and Diminishers and will present the five disciplines of the Multiplier. You will read stories of real Multipliers and Diminishers; be aware that we've changed the Diminishers' names (and companies) for rather obvious reasons. The book concludes with a road map for becoming a Multiplier.

MY CHALLENGE TO YOU

Although the Multiplier/Diminisher framework might appear binary, I wish to emphasize that there is a continuum between Multipliers and Diminishers, with just a small number of people at either polar extreme. Our research showed that most of us fall along this spectrum and have the ability to move toward the side of the Multiplier. With the right intent, the Multiplier approach to leadership can be developed. The good news is that 1) Multipliers are out there, 2) we have studied them to uncover their secrets, and 3) you can learn to become one. And not only can you become a Multiplier yourself, you can find and create other Multipliers. That will make you a multiplier of Multipliers.

It is within this context that I challenge you to read this book at several levels. At the most fundamental level, you might read it to illuminate what you undoubtedly have experienced—that some leaders create genius while others destroy it. Or you might go beyond this and read to reflect on the quintessential Multipliers and Diminishers that have been part of your career and life experience. But perhaps the best way to approach this book is to look beyond the idea that you or your colleagues are Multipliers, and instead spot yourself at times in the anatomy of a Diminisher. The greatest power of these ideas might be in realizing that you have the mind of a Multiplier but that you've been living in a Diminisher world and you've lost your way. Perhaps you are an Accidental Diminisher.

As Greg and I have journeyed into the world of Multipliers and Diminishers, we have often seen glimpses of ourselves—either in the present or from years past—and have found ways to better exemplify the Multiplier in our own work teaching and coaching leaders around the world.

The book is a guide to those of you who wish to follow the path of the Multiplier and, like British Prime Minister Benjamin Disraeli, leave those you meet thinking they, rather than you, are the smartest person in the world. It is a book for executives who want to seed their organization with more Multipliers and watch everyone and everything get better.

Let me now introduce you to the fascinating and diverse set of leaders we call the Multipliers. They come from all walks of life—from corporate board rooms, to our schools' classrooms, and from the Oval Office to the fields of Africa. We've selected leaders who represent diverse ideologies. I encourage you to learn from everyone, even those whose political views you do not share. I hope you will find their stories, their practices, and their impact as inspiring as we did when we entered their worlds.

THE MULTIPLIER FORMULA

MULTIPLIERS VERSUS DIMINISHERS

MULTIPLIERS: These leaders are genius makers and bring out the intelligence in others. They build collective, viral intelligence in organizations.

DIMINISHERS: These leaders are absorbed in their own intelligence, stifle others, and deplete the organization of crucial intelligence and capability.

The Five Disciplines of the Multipliers

1. *The Talent Magnet:* Attract and optimize talent
2. *The Liberator:* Require people's best thinking
3. *The Challenger:* Extend challenges
4. *The Debate Maker:* Debate decisions
5. *The Investor:* Instill accountability

The Results

By extracting people's full capability, Multipliers get twice the capability from people than do Diminishers.

CHAPTER 2

THE TALENT MAGNET

I not only use all the brains that I have,
but all that I can borrow.

WOODROW WILSON

When you walk up to the porch of her house in Menlo Park, California, you can sense that Meg Whitman, CEO of eBay, has spent time on the East Coast. With its saltbox shape and white wood, it is one of those West Coast houses that looks like it should be in New England. The house just might remind Meg of her time in Cambridge, Massachusetts, while at business school.

It was September 2007, and early in the race for the 2008 presidential nomination. There were many interesting candidates vying for the ticket for both parties. That day was a chance for us locals to get a peek at one of the candidates, and for me, it was a chance to extend our research and gain insight into two interesting leaders.

As the guests gathered on her backyard lawn, Meg Whitman took the microphone and began to introduce Mitt Romney as a candidate for president of the United States. Her introduction was simple.

> *I was a young consultant at Bain & Company and had the good*
> *fortune to work for Mitt Romney early in my career. After we were*
> *hired, all the new consultants scrambled to get on Mitt's project*

*teams. Why? The word spread that he was the best boss to work
for because he knew how to lead a team and he grew his people.
Everyone grew around Mitt.*

You can imagine Meg, a newly minted Harvard MBA, ready to
make her mark on the business world. Like many MBAs, she chose
to begin her career at Bain & Company, an elite business consulting
firm. But she knew landing in the right place inside would determine
how quickly she'd learn and advance her career and her value in the
marketplace. She heard from one of the more senior consultants, "If
you're smart, you'll find a spot on Mitt Romney's team." She didn't
quite know why Mitt was such a great boss, but being savvy, she ma-
neuvered her way onto his team. She learned why when she started
working with him.

On Mitt's team, people were engaged. He took the time to get to
know each person and to understand the capabilities they brought to
the team. This went well beyond reviewing their resume. Mitt would
determine what people were naturally good at and find a way to use
those talents with the client engagement. In assigning people to roles,
Mitt asked questions like "What is the next challenge for you? What
would be a stretch assignment?" It wasn't unusual for someone on
Mitt's team to get loaned to another group if their skills could help
rescue a troubled project. In one-on-one meetings, Mitt not only
asked about the status of project deliverables, he asked about the
blockers. A favorite question was "What is getting in the way of your
being successful?"

Meanwhile, many of Meg's colleagues didn't get the same guidance and found themselves working for more typical company leaders
who appeared more concerned with advancing their own careers than
growing the people on their team. Team meetings typically consisted
of long briefings from project leaders, followed by the usual project
updates from each of the consultants who reported on progress in
their functional area. People stuck to their roles on the team. When

one person was struggling, he or she usually just suffered in silence and pulled a few all-nighters rather than relying on help from colleagues. The job got done, but individual efforts were not acknowledged. The only visible recognition was kudos given to the project leader and an increase in the size of his or her organization. As for the destiny of the project members, they were almost certainly guaranteed a role on the next project that closely resembled what they had done on the last project.

In any organization, there are Talent Magnets, people who attract the best talent, utilize it to its fullest, and ready it for the next stage. These are leaders who have a reputation not only for delivering results, but for creating a place where young, talented people can grow. They are accelerators to other people's careers.

Mitt Romney operated as a Talent Magnet. He accelerated the career of Meg Whitman, who went on to be CEO of eBay and lead an eighty-eight times increase in revenue. Not only did he have this impact on Meg, Mitt was a magnet and an accelerator in the careers of hundreds of people with a similar story.

Perhaps you are a Talent Magnet. Would your people describe you as someone who recognizes talented people, draws them in, and utilizes them at their fullest? Would they say they have grown more around you than any other manager they have worked for? Or would they describe you as someone who pulled them into your organization not as a talent to be developed, but more as a resource to be deployed and then left to languish? Or would they perhaps say that they were heavily recruited but not given a meaningful role—rather just a visible role, and served as a showpiece or hood ornament in your organization?

Some leaders are like magnets that draw in talent and develop it to its fullest. Other leaders acquire resources to build their empire. This chapter explores the difference in these two approaches to the management of talent and the impact that these leaders have on the people around them.

THE EMPIRE BUILDER VERSUS
THE TALENT MAGNET

Multipliers operate as Talent Magnets. They attract talented people and then use them to their fullest; you might think of it as working at their highest point of contribution. They get access to the best talent, not because they are necessarily great recruiters, but rather because people flock to work for them. As Meg Whitman found Mitt Romney, people seek out a Talent Magnet. They do so knowing their capabilities will be appreciated and knowing their value will also appreciate in the marketplace.

In contrast, Diminishers operate as Empire Builders who hoard resources and underutilize talent. They bring in top talent and make big promises, but they underutilize their people and disenchant them. Why? Because they are often amassing the resources for self-promotion and their own gain. Empire builders accumulate people. They collect people like knickknacks in a curio cabinet—on display for everyone to see, but not well utilized.

Each of these approaches produces a self-perpetuating cycle. The Talent Magnet spawns a virtuous cycle of attraction and the Empire Builder spawns a vicious cycle of decline.

A Cycle of Attraction

In 1914, Ernest Shackleton, the venerated British explorer, embarked on an expedition to traverse Antarctica. His recruitment advertisement in *The Times* (London) read:

> *Men wanted: For hazardous journey. Small wages, bitter cold, long months of complete darkness, constant danger, safe return doubtful. Honour and recognition in case of success.*

Surprisingly, hundreds of men applied. Shackleton, with the wisdom of an experienced captain, staffed his crew with men of a certain orientation—men who were attracted to adventure and recognition but who were also realistically prepared for the hardship they would face. No doubt Shackleton's ability to attract the right team was one key factor in the survival of every member of the expedition.

The cycle of attraction begins with a leader possessing the confidence and magnetism to surround him or herself with "*A players*"—sheer raw talent and the right mix of intelligence needed for the challenge. Under the leadership of the Talent Magnet, the genius of these players gets discovered and utilized to the fullest. Having been stretched, these players become smarter and more capable. *A* players become *A+* players. These people are positioned in the spotlight and get kudos and recognition for their work. They attract attention and their value increases in the talent marketplace, internally or externally. These *A+* players get offered even bigger opportunities and seize them with the full support of the Talent Magnet.

And then the cycle kicks into hyperdrive. As this pattern of utilization, growth, and opportunity occurs across multiple people, others in the organization notice and the leader and the organization get a reputation. They build a reputation as a "the place to grow." This reputation spreads and more *A* players flock to work in the Talent Magnet's organization, so there is a steady flow of talent in the door, replacing talent growing out of the organization.

This cycle of attraction, outlined below, is exactly what happened to Mitt Romney at Bain & Company and why Meg Whitman knew to join his organization.

THE CYCLE OF ATTRACTION

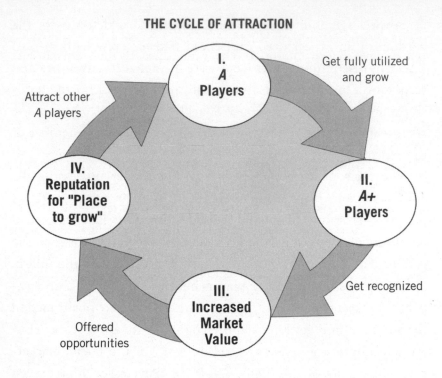

A Talent Magnet creates a powerful force that attracts talent and then accelerates the growth of intelligence and capability. These leaders operate like an electromagnetic force that, through interactions between atoms, propels matter in the universe.

A Cycle of Decline

For many years, I had the pleasure of working closely with a colleague named Brian Beckham[1], a brilliant and affable Canadian. Brian had a reputation for being smart, optimistic, and collaborative, and could solve just about any complex problem that got tossed his way. This reputation earned him a key role as the vice president of operations in a rapidly growing division. The problem was that the division was run by an uncontrolled Diminisher and determined Empire Builder.

Brian went to work solving the complex problems of the emerging division; however, he soon found that the SVP running the division didn't really want the underlying issues addressed. The SVP wanted one thing: Grow an empire! And he wanted growth at all costs. Brian's role quickly degenerated into window dressing, where he and his team fixed issues on the surface, just enough so the executive committee would continue to fund additional headcount into the organization. For many months, Brian continued to pursue his work at full throttle, but deep problems were festering at the core of the division. With continued indifference from his manager, Brian became numb and started to settle into mediocrity. He lost good players on his team. When other leaders in the company saw the depth of the problems in this division, Brian's Midas-touch reputation quickly tarnished. After several years hanging in there hoping for things to improve, he found himself stuck in a dying organization, watching his opportunities fade.

Soon Brian became one of the walking dead that roam the halls of so many organizations. On the outside, these zombies go through the motions, but on the inside they have given up. They "quit and stay." It was painful to watch this happen to Brian, whom I knew to be an absolute superstar. No doubt you have seen this happen to colleagues in other organizations or have even been there yourself. Is it possible that it is happening inside your own organization?

Empire Builders create a vicious cycle of decline. Talent recruited into their organization soon becomes disengaged and goes stale. The cycle of decline begins much like the cycle of attraction (which is why it is easy to be deceived by Diminishers). Empire Builders seek to surround themselves with A players. But unlike Talent Magnets, they accumulate talent to appear smarter and more powerful. The leader glosses over the real genius of the people while placing them into boxes on the org chart. The A players have limited impact and start to look more like A– or B+. They fail to get noticed for their work, and they lose intellectual confidence. They begin to recede into the shadow of the Empire Builder. Their value in the job market drops and opportunities begin to evaporate. So they stay and wait, hoping things will turn around. This cycle of degeneration impacts not only one person; it infects an entire organization. The organization becomes an elephant graveyard earning a reputation as "the place people go to die." As one technology superstar said of his empty vice president job, "I'm definitely past my sell-by date here." The resignation in his voice made it clear: if he were milk, he'd be curdled.

Empire Builders, having earned their reputation as career killers, continually struggle to get truly top talent into their organizations. Perhaps this is why they labor hard to hoard the resources that they have. Empire Builders may initially be able to attract top talent, but their focus on building themselves and their organizations underutilizes the true talent that they have in their organization and renders it stagnant and inert.

They generate a cycle of decline that spirals downward as illustrated below.

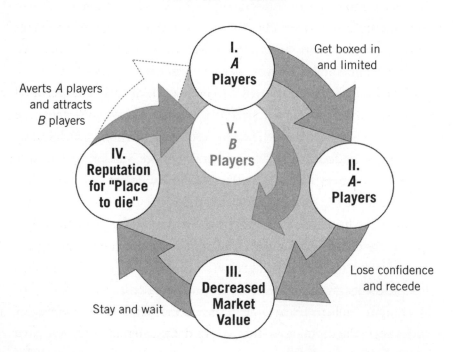

THE CYCLE OF DECLINE

Empire Builders hoard resources and underutilize talent. Talent Magnets attract talented people and use them at their highest point of contribution. Let's explore the world of the Talent Magnet, these Multipliers who create a cycle of attraction and grow intelligence around them.

THE TALENT MAGNET

The Talent Magnet creates a cycle of attraction that accelerates performance and grows genius. But does this only work for top talent and for the *A* players in the market? Or can a true Talent Magnet find and grow genius everywhere and with everyone?

Hexal AG, a maker of generic drugs, is located in a small village close to Munich, Germany. Hexal was founded in 1986 by twin brothers and self-made entrepreneurs, Thomas and Andreas Strüengmann. Andreas, a doctor, is the medical authority and Thomas is the international marketing genius behind Hexal. These brothers teamed their expertise to build a successful generic drug company, growing primarily from the local talent pool in the village. What makes the company unique is that its approach to talent is anything but generic. It is an approach that gets extraordinary results from very ordinary people. It starts with how these leaders hire people into their company.

Anyone who has been in the hiring manager's seat knows the process can be painful. To find the right candidate, you know you will waste a lot of time interviewing the wrong candidates. This is particularly frustrating because you typically know they are the wrong candidate in the first three minutes of a job interview. But regardless, you feel compelled to proceed with the obligatory sixty-minute interview and the pleasantries of "We'll get back to you."

The Strüengmann brothers cut right to the chase. When they were looking for a general manager for Hexal in the Netherlands, they began with the normal actions—they engaged an external recruiter, gave her the job requirements, and then waited for a list of candidates. The recruiter brought forward nine candidates. But then they did something quite unusual. They made arrangements to conduct the interviews in a single day in a rented conference room at Schiphol Airport, just outside Amsterdam. The recruiter reviewed their planned interview schedule and was shocked—they had allowed just ten minutes per interview. She called to inform them that it was impossible to interview so quickly! The Strüengmann brothers disagreed. They met with each candidate for just three minutes—every candidate except their final candidate, with whom they spent three hours. They explained their unusual approach: "When we consider each person, we ask one or two questions. If they don't fit, we simply don't continue the conversation. If the person is individualistic, we know that he or she won't fit in our culture. When we find someone who will fit with our company, then we spend a lot of time with this person to make sure we understand their capability and what they would bring to our organization." The Strüengmann brothers knew how to spot and attract the right talent.

Once people joined Hexal, they discovered another one of the Strüengmanns' unconventional practices. Hexal doesn't have jobs per se, and they don't have an org chart. This isn't like some elite organizations that choose not to publish their org chart for fear that some other company will snatch up their talent. Hexal didn't have an org chart because the Strüengmanns didn't believe in them. Jobs were loosely created around people's interests and unique capabilities. They called their approach the "ameba model." Here's how it works.

Ursula's responsibility was to assist the customer services manager. In her role, she saw a large number of repetitive requests for the same action and was continually updating people on the status of these requests. She had an idea to use the Internet to create a workflow tracking system. She wrote up a little proposal and sent the idea around to her colleagues in an e-mail asking, "What do you think about it?" Some people replied on e-mail and others stopped by her desk to discuss it in person, but everyone agreed that it was a good idea and wanted to see it happen. She gathered the people she needed, secured some budget, and got the system built through this makeshift team. The team then presented the system to the Strüengmann brothers, who applauded their efforts and Ursula's leadership and initiative. These twin brothers simply believed that if an idea got support from a lot of people, it was a good idea. At Hexal, you could work wherever there was energy.

Through encouraging their employees to use this heat-seeking approach, they were able to utilize people at their highest point of contribution. They didn't box people into jobs and limit their contribution. They let people work where they had ideas and energy and where they could best contribute. They let talent flow, like an ameba, to the right opportunities.

There are clearly multiple reasons for their success, but it is interesting to note that the Strüengmann brothers sold Hexal (along with holdings in another company) to Novartis in 2005 for $7.6 billion; at age fifty-five, they were each worth $3.8 billion. As they lead Hexal, the Strüengmann brothers got extraordinary results from very ordinary people. Why? Because these twin Talent Magnets knew how to unleash people's genius into their organization.

How does a Talent Magnet find and unleash genius? In the four practices of the Talent Magnet, we find some of the answers.

THE FOUR PRACTICES OF THE TALENT MAGNET

Among the Multipliers we studied in our research, we found four active practices that together catalyze and sustain this cycle of attraction. These Talent Magnets: 1) look for talent everywhere; 2) find people's native genius; 3) utilize people at their fullest; and 4) remove the blockers. Let's look at each to understand exactly what a Talent Magnet does to create genius in others.

I. Look for Talent Everywhere

Talent Magnets are always looking for new talent, and they look far beyond their own backyard. Multipliers cast a wide net and find talent in many settings and diverse forms, knowing that intelligence has many facets.

Appreciate All Types of Genius

In 1904, a test of intelligence that later evolved into the IQ test was developed by French researcher Alfred Binet as a tool for assessing the learning progress of French schoolchildren. His assumption was that lower intelligence signaled a need for more and different teaching, not an inability to learn.[2] This tool quickly became ubiquitous as a unilateral determinant of intellectual horsepower. Much work has been done over the last two decades by cognitive psychologists around the world, offering additional methods for identifying and developing intelligence. Whether it is Harvard professor Howard Gardner's theory of multiple intelligences, Daniel Goleman's work on emotional intelligence, or Stanford professor Carol Dweck's work on the effect of mindsets on capability, the message is clear: IQ is a practical but limited measure of the true intelligence of our species. We are simply smarter in more ways than can be measured through an IQ test.

A Talent Magnet knows that genius comes in many forms. Some minds excel at quantitative analysis or verbal reasoning—capabilities measured through IQ, SAT, and other tests of traditional cognitive intelligence. Other minds offer creative genius, innovating through fresh thinking and bold ideas. Some minds are critical, spotting every problem or landmine lurking within a plan; the genius of some others is to find a way to tunnel around these landmines.

Bill Campbell, former CEO of Intuit, is one such leader who appreciates the diversity of talent requisite to build a successful company. This economics major and football coach at Columbia University is renowned for his ability to lead and guide Silicon Valley's elite technologists. Bill reflects, "Their minds can do something that mine can't.

They have a genius that I don't." He communicates this respect for the intelligence of others through his actions. He readily admits that he doesn't think like they do and that he appreciates what they bring to the table. He listens intently to the ideas and advice of those who offer this perspective he doesn't have. And he asks people to teach him what he doesn't know. This rich appreciation for the genius of others is how this former football coach has become a personal advisor to the CEOs at Apple, Google, and many more.

Ignore Boundaries

In their quest to assemble the finest talent, Talent Magnets are blind to organizational boundaries. They see the multiple forms of intelligence that exist everywhere. Talent Magnets live in a world without walls and without hierarchical or lateral restrictions. Instead, they see talent networks.

You can often spot Talent Magnets inside organizations because they are the ones who ignore org charts. Org charts are handy for finding out who works for whom and who's in charge if something goes wrong, but these issues are of relative unimportance when you are searching for genius. As far as Talent Magnets are concerned, org charts are irrelevant. Why? Because, *everyone* works for them—or at least every person whose genius they can uncover. The mind of the Multiplier works like this: *If I can find someone's genius, I can put them to work.*

The idea is simple. Multipliers understand that people love to contribute their genius. If they put in the effort to figure out someone's genius, they have opened a pathway for that person to contribute. They can utilize them. Multipliers aren't deterred if someone doesn't officially report to them on an org chart. These leaders see an unlimited talent pool that they can draw from. Everyone works for a Multiplier.

For this reason, you can often spot Multipliers leading cross-functional projects and intercompany ventures. They may be in key staff roles, or they may also be at the top of the org chart. The common denominator is that they look beyond boundaries for talent.

Zvi Schreiber, CEO of G.ho.st, is one such Talent Magnet. Zvi, the company's British-born Israeli chief executive, started G.ho.st with the ambition of providing users with a free Web-based virtual computer that lets them access their desktop and files from any computer with an Internet connection. His business strategy was to break down walls in the computing world. He called the company G.ho.st for Global Hosted Operating System, because ghosts can go through walls.

Zvi took a similar approach to finding the talent he needed to build his company. Headquartered in Modiin, Israel, Zvi could have easily built the company with the abundant supply of technical and business talent in Israel. But he could see a rich supply of technically savvy talent in Palestine that became isolated by failed peace agreements. Zvi convinced his venture partner, Benchmark Capital, to make a risky move and support him in building a company that spanned the Israeli-Palestinian divide.

The Palestinian office in Ramallah, West Bank, houses about thirty-five software developers and is responsible for most of the research and programming. The Israeli team is smaller and works about thirteen miles away in the Israeli town of Modiin. The team works through video conferencing. When face-to-face meetings are necessary, colleagues gather at a run-down coffee shop on a desert road near Jericho, frequented by camels and Bedouin shepherds.[3]

This Talent Magnet not only looked beyond the fabricated borders of organizational structure to find the best talent to staff his company. The boundaries he broke through, borders steeped in cultural, political and physical conflict, were patrolled by armed guards.

Talent Magnets look for talent everywhere and then study that talent to uncover and unlock the real genius that lies within.

II. Find People's Native Genius

As the head of a global function inside a multinational corporation, I spent a lot of time in cross-functional meetings and on task forces. It was almost inevitable that at some point in these meetings, when things would become murky, someone would hand me the whiteboard pen, point to the front of the room, and say, "Liz, lead us through this." I'd readily jump in and do my thing, and hand back the pen at some point. After a while, I started to wonder why I almost never got to be a regular meeting attendee and sit in the back of the room and check e-mail. I thought, *Why do I always get asked to lead these difficult meetings? Why am I always getting put in charge when it isn't even my job?* After seeing this pattern repeated over many years at work and in other group settings, I realized that I wasn't being asked to be in charge per se—it was a very particular type of "in charge." I would find myself in charge when a group needed more of a facilitative leader and less of a boss. I vividly remember one of my colleagues trying to explain to me why I was always getting asked to lead these types of meetings. Ben explained, "It is because you can so easily frame the issue, synthesize what people are saying, and lay out a course of action." What? I stared at him blankly, trying to decipher what he was saying. It sounded like he was telling me that I was good at breathing. It didn't strike me as a particularly big deal or something someone might find difficult. It *was* as easy as breathing; at least it was for me. What my colleagues were teaching me was that I had a native ability—something that I did both easily and freely.

Look for What Is Native

Talent Magnets know how to uncover and access the native genius of others. By "native genius" I mean something even more specific than a strength or a skill that might be highly rated on a 360 degree leadership assessment. A native genius is something that people do, not only exceptionally well, but absolutely naturally. They do it easily (without extra effort) and freely (without condition).

What people do easily, they do without conscious effort. They do it better than anything else they do, but they don't need to apply extraordinary effort to the task. They get results that are head-and-shoulders above others but they do it without breaking a sweat.

What people do freely, they do without condition. They don't need to be paid or rewarded, and they often don't even need to be asked. It is something that gives them inherent satisfaction, and they offer their capability voluntarily, even ardently. It is effortless, and they stand ready and willing to contribute, whether it is a formal job requirement or not.

Finding someone's native genius is the key that unlocks discretionary effort. It propels people to go beyond what is required and offer their full intelligence. Finding people's genius begins by carefully observing them in action, looking for spikes of authentic enthusiasm and a natural flow of energy. As you watch someone in action, ask these questions:

- What do they do better than anything else they do?

- What do they do better than the people around them?

- What do they do without effort?

- What do they do without being asked?

- What do they do readily without being paid?

Label It

Native genius can be so instinctive for people that they may not even understand their own capability. Perhaps you've heard the phrase "fish discover water last." But if people aren't aware of their genius, they are not in a position to deliberately utilize it. By telling people what you see, you can raise their awareness and confidence, allowing them to provide their capability more fully.

Players for Larry Gelwix, head coach of the almost unbeatable Highland High School rugby team, often report that he got more out of them than other coaches. Consider one specific player, John. Before working with Larry, John saw himself as a good athlete but not a great one. But Larry pointed out something that changed his view of himself.

John recalled, "Larry commented publicly about my speed." John was surprised when the coach started talking in front of the other guys about how fast he was. He continued, "I thought I had good speed, but not great speed. But because Larry singled it out, it inspired me to develop a distinct self-concept: *I was fast.* And every time I found myself in a situation where speed was required, I remembered this, and I pushed myself beyond my limits." John not only became fast, he became really fast.

By labeling his genius for him, Larry unlocked this ability for John. Like John, people's first reaction to hearing someone describe a genius of theirs can often be bemusement. You know you've hit a genius nerve when they say, "Really? Can't everyone do this?" or "But this is no big deal!" Finding people's native genius and then labeling it is a direct approach to drawing more intelligence from them.

III. Utilize People at Their Fullest

Once a Talent Magnet has uncovered the native genius of others, he or she looks for opportunities that demand that capability. Some of these are obvious; others require a fresh look at the business or the organization. Once they've engaged the person's true genius, they shine a spotlight on them so other people can see their genius in action.

Connect People with Opportunities

Peter Merrill was a college student hired in a $9-an-hour part-time position as a front-line customer service representative for a professional coaching firm. He took more calls than the average rep and had an almost perfect record of "saving" customers who called in ready to cancel out of their programs.

What would a typical manager do with someone like Peter? Make sure he was happy? Perhaps offer him a full-time job upon graduation? Such a course of action would cement his current level of contribution within the firm and position him, in time, for a promotion.

But Ann Khalsa, Peter's manager's manager, wasn't happy with that posture. She dug a little deeper. Peter appeared good at saving customers, but why? It turned out to be what Ann called a "listening spike," by which she meant he listened to customers so sincerely and so thoughtfully, they would volunteer to give the company another chance.

But her curiosity continued. Why was he so good at listening to people? It turned out he had a particular aptitude and interest in helping people break through to the next level in their lives and careers. She tested her hypothesis with people who worked with Peter, and they agreed. They said that his conversation always tilted in that direction—even on lunch breaks.

The question for Ann became where to best utilize Peter. She knew he could do good work in customer service, and she gave him reign to make rapid changes there. But she also consciously identified several roles within the company where he could operate at a higher point of contribution.

Within three weeks of being hired in customer service, at Ann's request, Peter was transferred to the coaching department to work with the company's toughest clients. In that role he earned more and contributed more as he achieved, amazingly, a zero cancellation rate. But Ann kept tabs on Peter, trying to figure out what opportunity would further increase Peter's personal net worth while providing significantly more value to the organization.

She cracked the code when she mentioned to Peter that he might want to set up a product line based on the ideas he had developed in his coaching work. He went from being a strong individual contributor to a successful leader within the company. Twelve months from the time he was hired as a part-time customer service representative, Peter launched the highest-margin product in the company, adding $2 million in annual revenue to the company. The difference is more than a tenfold increase in value from the same employee.

This art of connecting people's genius to opportunities that allow them to be used at their highest point of contribution is a natural but deliberate management approach for Ann. She doesn't need to take her team to offsite meetings to analyze their different personality types. Instead, she watches people until she has an idea of what they do effortlessly and what area they are naturally drawn to. Then she has an ongoing conversation with herself about where this person's aptitude could benefit the company.

Could there be people in your customer service department who would produce a million dollars in value if they were unleashed on the right opportunity? Are there people on your team who are being blocked from working at a higher point of contribution?

Shine a Spotlight

Each summer in the Sierra Mountains of California, roughly seventy-five teenage girls eagerly gather for an annual girls' camp—a week of fun, adventure, and camaraderie that often serves as a watershed event in their young lives. The camp is run entirely on the volunteer efforts of sixty leaders. For the last six years, Marguerite Hancock has served (also as a volunteer) as the camp director at the helm of this incredible group of youth and leaders.

Marguerite works as a Stanford University research director and teacher and is smart, accomplished, and extraordinarily capable. She is a strong leader with strong ideas of her own. One of her assistant directors said, "Marguerite is so capable, she could do virtually any aspect of girls' camp herself." But what is interesting about Marguerite isn't that she could—it is that she *doesn't*. Instead, she leads like a Multiplier, invoking brilliance and dedication in the other fifty-nine leaders who make this camp a reality.

Marguerite begins by building a "dream team" carefully recruited for each person's individual strengths. One of the assistant directors said, "Marguerite studies people. She watches them until she figures out what they are great at. She chose her assistant directors not only for their strengths but because we each had strengths in areas where she was weak." She then finds a place where each person's strengths will shine. For some, it is working with the girls one-on-one; for another, it is managing the sports program; for another it is leading the nightly campfire. But each role is carefully cast to draw upon the unique talents of every person on the team.

Marguerite then makes it clear to each person why she has been selected for that role. She not only notices their talent; she labels it for them. One camp leader said, "She tells me the talent she sees in me and why it matters. She tells me why girls' camp will be better because of me and my work." But Marguerite doesn't stop there. She lets everyone else know, too. It is typical for her to introduce someone to the group by saying, "This is Jennifer. She's a creative genius, and we are so fortunate to have her leading our art program."

With her cast of talent assembled, Marguerite then goes to the back of the room, takes control of the spotlight, and begins shining it on others. She is effusive with praise, but it is never empty. Her praise of others' work is specific, and it is public. The other leaders at camp can see the direct link between their work and the success of the camp. A camp leader said, "She not only tells you that you are doing a great job, but she tells you why it matters to these girls. I know my work is appreciated."

Marguerite finds other people's genius and then shines a spotlight on it for everyone to see their talent in action. What is the result? A character-building, life-changing experience for seventy-five young women, but also a deeply rewarding, growing experience for the fifty-nine leaders who serve along with Marguerite.

IV. Remove the Blockers

Talent Magnets are attracters and growers of talent and intelligence. Leaders who serve as Multipliers provide both the space and the resources to yield this growth. But Talent Magnets go beyond just giving people resources. They remove the impediments, which quite often means removing the people who are blocking and impeding the growth of others. In almost every organization there are people who overrun others, consuming the resources needed to fuel the growth of people around them. Like weeds in a garden bed, they choke the development of the intelligence around them.

Get Rid of Prima Donnas

Bloom Energy, located in the heart of Silicon Valley, had developed a fuel cell system that produces clean, reliable, and affordable energy. As venture capital firm Kleiner Perkins Caulfield & Byers's first green-tech venture, Bloom Energy has become a leader in their industry. Leading Bloom Energy is K.R. Sridhar, renowned aerospace and environmental scientist and an energy thought leader.

When K.R. Sridhar started Bloom Energy, he began with what he calls "gene pool engineering." K.R. explains, "A players attract other A players. Their smarts and passion make other smart, passionate people want to work here. So your first fifty employees are the most important, and hardest." When Bloom Energy needed to hire their first fifty employees, there was no established green-tech industry at the time. So K.R. broke down each technology they would require to build their energy generators and identified the leading company in this technology. He then researched and found the person inside each company that the company would least want to lose. He reached out to these people, explained the bold challenge Bloom Energy was undertaking, and recruited them to join the company. He engineered a gene pool of elite technical talent who were the best in their respective fields. He now had the talent he needed, and the work of building a team that would deliver an integrated energy technology began. He established one rule: No prima donnas—leave your ego at the door and work as a team.

Within this elite team, one technologist was particularly indispensable. Stefan, an outstanding scientist, was the world expert in the technology that was the lynchpin in their solution. As the team worked, it became clear that Stefan couldn't collaborate and had become entrenched in his position about the technical direction the company should pursue.

Tensions mounted in the team because the company had just committed to an important beta release in eighteen months. K.R. pulled Stefan into his office and explained the situation, but Stefan wouldn't back down. Knowing how essential he was to the technical viability of the venture, he made it clear to K.R.: it was either him or the team. K.R. explained the options, but Stefan's ego wouldn't allow him to let go of the issue.

K.R. contemplated the issue and the risks involved. Within the hour, he had made his decision. He chose the team. He walked Stefan to the door, then walked over to the rest of the team and explained his actions. "I have put us at significant risk, but I know we have it in us to overcome this. I trust that we will get through this, but there will be significant delays," he explained. Initially the group was silent, stunned that K.R. was willing to let go of their top technologist. One team member broke the silence and said, "There will be no delays. We will do things we have never done before to get this done." With renewed energy, the team worked weekends and extraordinary hours. They brought in consultants with the critical expertise they lacked. They kept up the pace for eighteen months while people grew to fill in the gap that was created by Stefan's departure. They delivered the product successfully, missing their original deadline by only two days!

This incident became the foundation for how the company would operate: the best talent in the industry, but not a single prima donna. Today, Bloom Energy is thriving and is often cited as the reason Kleiner Perkins continues to expand their green-tech portfolio.

K.R. Sridhar accelerated the development of the intellectual assets of this company by getting rid of the prima donna who was impeding the intelligence of the whole organization.

A CEO of a $3 billion consumer products firm was leading his management team through an important product pricing decision that had the potential to generate profits that would fund much-needed R&D expenditures. One member of the management team, Ron, was reluctant to let go of the current model and to support the direction of the team. After a series of management meetings to debate the issues, it came down to a moment-of-truth decision in an important executive staff meeting. Prior to the meeting, the CEO pulled Ron aside and asked frankly, "If the team wants to move forward with the pricing change, will you let go of your position against this and support a new model?" Ron agreed that he would support the new direction.

However, during the staff meeting, Ron again dug in his heels, telling the group, "My team simply won't support this new pricing model." There was a silent exasperation in the room as the team could see that their ideas and energy were being blocked once again. The CEO stopped the meeting and asked Ron to step outside. He took him about forty yards down the hall to his office and he fired him. Right there on the spot.

As he walked back to the conference room, the CEO wondered if he had acted too fast and if this move would throw off the team. He reentered the conference room and told them. Instead of concern, he could see relief on their faces. One executive team member said, "Look, if anything, I think you waited too long."

Is it possible that your smartest people may be impeding the smarts of your organization? And is it possible you are waiting too long to remove the blockers?

Get Out of the Way

Sometimes a Talent Magnet removes the prima donna who is blocking the intelligence of others. But sometimes the blocker is the leader him- or herself. C.K. Prahalad, management guru and one of my mentors, once shared with me an old saying in India: "Nothing grows under a banyan tree." It provides shade and is comfortable, but it allows no sun in for growth. Many leaders are banyan trees; they protect their people, but nothing grows under them.

One corporate VP had a favorite saying, quoted often and written on her door: "Ignore me as needed to get your job done." This simple mantra signaled an important trust in the judgment and capability of others. Her people knew that exercising their judgment and getting the job done rapidly was more important than placating the boss. She told new staff members, "Yes, there will be a few times when I get agitated because I would have done it differently, but I'll get over it. I'd rather you trust your judgment, keep moving, and get the job done."

Talent Magnets remove the barriers that block the growth of intelligence in their people.

The world of the Talent Magnet is dynamic. Talent is drawn in by the strong gravitational pull of the Talent Magnet. It is then fully utilized, stretched, made continually ready for new challenges. Life with an Empire Builder doesn't offer the same thrill ride. It is a world of politics, ownership, and limitations.

THE DIMINISHER'S APPROACH
TO MANAGING TALENT

Multipliers operate from a belief that talent exists everywhere and they can use it at its highest if they can simply identify the genius in people. Diminishers think *People need to report to me in order to get them to do anything.* One such senior director said the only thing that was wrong with the underperforming IT division was that it reported to someone else. He saw owning the resources himself as the primary solution. Diminishers are owners of talent, not developers of talent. Because they don't actively develop talent, people in their organizations languish and can actually regress.

ACQUIRE RESOURCES. Empire Builders focus their energy on acquiring resources and slotting them into organizational structures where they are visible and clearly under the command of the leader. For some leaders, this amassing of talent can become an obsession.

Recall Jasper Wallis, the high-cost Diminisher from the first chapter, who was obsessed with the size of his organization relative to those of his peers on the executive team. After years of building his organization with his right hand while masking the underlying problems with his left hand, Jasper succeeded in building an empire complete with a separate office tower, customer visit center, and training campus just for his division. However, his organization had become gangly after such rapid, unrestrained growth and created additional problems of integration and coordination. The hole became deeper and deeper until the division was radically scaled back and folded into another group. Like ancient Rome, the empire eventually got overextended and collapsed under its own weight.

PUT PEOPLE IN BOXES. Divide and conquer is the modus operandi of Empire Builders. They bring in great talent and carve out a fiefdom for them, but they don't encourage people to step beyond these walls. Rather than give broad scope to their management team, Empire Builders ensure that they, themselves, are the point of integration. You can often spot an Empire Builder because he or she either operates exclusively through one-on-one meetings or runs staff meetings as an official report-out from each fiefdom.

One manager was known for making key decisions one-on-one rather than with his team. This fostered a covert and high-stakes game among his lieutenants. Each of them would vie for the coveted one-on-one meeting time—the last meeting on a Friday afternoon. Why? Because everyone knew that he made his decisions by himself over the weekend and announced them in his staff meeting on Monday. People quickly learned that the person who got his ear last on Friday afternoon would have the most influence. His divide-and-conquer approach not only kept people in narrowly defined roles, it was a dangerous and costly way to make decisions.

LET TALENT LANGUISH. One way Empire Builders stifle their talent is by hogging the limelight for themselves. They are often the prima donna, insisting that they get maximum time on the stage and that scripts are written to feature them. Whereas Talent Magnets give credit, Empire Builders take credit.

Hogging the limelight is an active way Empire Builders hold others back, but the more insidious problem is actually what they don't do. These managers actively acquire talent, but then are passive about growing it. They are, for the most part, oblivious to the development of others. In fact, in our quantitative research, we found that "develops the talent of the team" was among the lowest three skills of the Diminisher.

They also stifle talent because they don't clear away the dead wood. One Diminisher we studied was notorious for draining his organization through his inaction. People said, "He and his management team never made decisions. They didn't make waves, they just kept analyzing." Instead of firing toxic or ineffective leaders, he would slowly disable them. One observer noted, "It was torture to watch one of his staff get cut off. It was like a child pulling off the legs of a spider one by one and then watching it hobble away."

When leaders play the role of the Empire Builder, they bring in great resources, but they underutilize them because they fundamentally undervalue them. They continue to operate in a "one brain, many hands" organizational model that stunts the growth of both intelligence and talent around them. Diminishers build organizations where people go to die. This is why Diminishers are costly to organizations. The assets in their portfolio don't increase in value.

LEVERAGING TALENT

Marguerite Hancock, the girls' camp director discussed earlier, is known for getting the maximum effort from her team. Not only does she attract and develop a team of A players; this university professor-researcher expects A work from everyone. She isn't shy about asking others to do the really tough stuff. One team member said, "She asks you to do really hard things. But she makes it an act of service, not servitude. And she fully expects you to ask other people to do hard things, too."

Under Marguerite's leadership, people say they "execute to the maximum" and "do things they never thought they could do." When girls' camp is over each year, her fellow leaders confess to feeling a certain relief it is done. But, they say, "I feel like all that effort was worth it. I'm absolutely exhausted, but I am ready to do it again."

A players delivering *A* work, exhausted but ready to do it again: This is the way of the Talent Magnet. This is how, under their leadership, smart people get smarter. Talent Magnets go beyond attracting smart people into the organization. They also draw out that talent by connecting people with opportunities that allow them to operate at their highest point of contribution.

The following chart reflects why Empire Builders leave capability on the table while Talent Magnets create and grow intelligence all around them.

Empire Builders		Talent Magnets	
What They Do	*What They Get*	*What They Do*	*What They Get*
Hoard resources and underutilize talent	A reputation as the person *A* players should avoid working for ("the place you go to die")	Attract talent and deploy it at its highest point of contribution	A reputation as the person *A* players should work for ("the place you go to grow")
	Underutilized people whose capability atrophies		Fully utilized people whose genius continues to expand
	Disillusioned *A* players who don't reach out to other *A* players		Inspired *A* players who attract other *A* players into the organization
	A stagnation of talent where disillusioned *A* players quit and stay		A flow of *A* players attracting other *A* players as they then move up and out of the organization

BECOMING A TALENT MAGNET

The promise of a Multiplier is that they get twice the capacity, plus a growth dividend from their people as their genius expands under the leadership of the Multiplier. Let's now look at a few starting points for becoming a Talent Magnet.

The Starting Block

BECOME A GENIUS WATCHER. Todd Paletta, a retailing executive and aspiring Multiplier, had just finished an exhausting business meeting in New York and settled into his business class seat, headed for home on the West Coast. As the plane took off, he heard the cry of a baby. He hoped it would stop after the plane settled into the standard cruising altitude of 30,000 feet. It didn't. He then realized the sound was right behind him—right there in business class. A baby in business class! The mother stood up in the aisle, trying to console the child. Now the jarring sound was right next to his ear. Todd was annoyed at first. But as his attention became focused on the mother, he started genius watching. He found himself studying her actions closely and appreciating her efforts to soothe the child. He observed the way she juggled the demands of the child and the silent frustrations of the other passengers. He watched longer and noticed her patience. He began talking with her, learning more about her, her efforts, and her interests. He started forming hypotheses about her talents and perhaps even a source of her genius. He then started to wonder, "If she worked on my team, how would I put these capabilities to use? Where would she excel?"

No, Todd didn't make a job offer to this mother during the flight, or after. The point is that Todd was learning to genius watch and was practicing it in even the most unusual of places and circumstances. He had spent the last two weeks studying the capabilities of the people in his organization, looking to identify their native genius and how he might best utilize it in his business. He was in genius-watching mode and he couldn't help but see it everywhere—even in the efforts of a mother with an inconsolable child and a plane full of aggravated passengers.

Here are three steps to help you begin genius watching:

1. *Identify it.* Make a list of eight to ten people you work with closely. Start to note the things they do both easily and freely. Go beyond surface-level skills like "she is an Excel spreadsheet wizard." If you need help finding the underlying capabilities, ask "why" about three times until you find the underlying capability that allows someone to do some activity well. For example, Susan may appear to be an Excel wizard on the surface, but perhaps it is because she is good at modeling data. And perhaps she is good at modeling data because she has a genius for critical thinking.

2. *Test it.* Once you've developed a hypothesis about each person, test out your thinking and refine your views. Ask a colleague if he thinks critical thinking is one of Susan's geniuses. Test the idea with Susan herself. Ask her what she is good at and what she wants to further excel at.

3. *Work it.* Once you've found a native genius for someone, make a list of five different roles you could put this person in that would utilize and expand this genius. If Susan is a financial analyst, what other roles could you put her in that would draw upon her intelligence for critical thinking? Perhaps she'd be good in a strategy role or on the marketing competitive intelligence team. Go beyond formal jobs and identify ad hoc roles. Perhaps Susan would be good at reviewing an important presentation that you are making to the board of directors to find holes or inconsistencies. Or maybe she should be assigned to a task force to pick the location of the next offshore R&D center. Just as the Talent Magnet looks for talent beyond organizational boundaries, look for jobs and roles both inside and outside of your organization.

PULL SOME WEEDS. Individual genius can be deceptive. At first look, it would appear costly to remove one supersmart player, even if she has a diminishing effect on a team. But one needs only to do the math to see the high cost of destructive genius. Our research consistently confirmed that Diminishers cause people to operate at about 50 percent of their full intelligence and capability. Removing a highly intelligent employee or leader can be difficult, but it can have huge payoffs. On a work team of eleven people, removing a Diminisher can give back the equivalent of five full-time people, with ten people operating at 100 percent. You may lose one mind, but you gain back five. It is a law of numbers.

Leaders most often know who the blockers are. The most common mistake they make is waiting too long to remove them. If you want to unleash the talent that is latent in your organization, find the weeds and pull them out. Don't do it quietly. Like K.R. Sridhar and the CEO described earlier, huddle the team immediately, and let them know that you've removed someone because he or she was holding back the team. Give people permission to think fully again.

Each of the above is a starting point that can create a proof point for the power of the Talent Magnet. Once successful, you will be one step further along the path of the Multiplier.

UP AND TO THE RIGHT

Sue Siegel, former president of Affymetrix and an extraordinary Multiplier, reflected on her pillar experiences as a leader. She said, "My best moments were when team members would call me after accomplishing some tough goal or overcoming a huge hurdle. They were usually tired, but they were brimming with enthusiasm, having grown through the challenge. These moments were exhilarating for them and me." The people who worked for Sue indeed describe the time as a highlight of their career.

Talent Magnets encourage people to grow and leave. They write letters of recommendation and they help people find their next stage to perform on. And when people leave their group, they celebrate their departures and shout their success to everyone. You see, these celebrations become their best recruiting tool.

Jack and Suzy Welch wrote, "The best thing about being a preferred employer is that it gets you good people, and this launches a virtuous cycle. The best team attracts the best team, and winning often leads to more winning. That's a ride that you and your employees will never want to get off."[4]

Talent Magnets create a cycle of attraction that is exhilarating for employer and employee alike. Their organizations are coveted places of employment, and people flock to work for them knowing the Talent Magnet will stretch them, grow them, and accelerate their careers. It is a thrill ride with the speed and exhilaration of a roller coaster but one that, like the revenue chart of every CFO's dreams, moves constantly "up and to the right."

THE MULTIPLIER FORMULA

THE EMPIRE BUILDER VERSUS THE TALENT MAGNET

EMPIRE BUILDERS bring in great talent, but they underutilize it because they hoard resources and use them only for their own gain.

TALENT MAGNETS get access to the best talent because people flock to work for them knowing they will be fully utilized and developed to be ready for the next stage.

The Four Practices of the Talent Magnet

1. *Look for Talent Everywhere*
   - Appreciate all types of genius
   - Ignore boundaries
2. *Find People's Native Genius*
   - Look for what is native
   - Label it
3. *Utilize People to Their Fullest*
   - Connect people with opportunities
   - Shine a spotlight
4. *Remove the Blockers*
   - Get rid of prima donnas
   - Get out of the way

Becoming a Talent Magnet

1. Become a genius watcher
2. Pull some weeds

Unexpected Findings

1. Both Talent Magnets and Empire Builders attract *A* talent. What differentiates them is what they do with the talent once it's in the door.

2. Talent Magnets don't run out of talent by moving their people on to bigger, better opportunities, because there is a steady stream of talent wanting to get into their organization.

CHAPTER 3

THE LIBERATOR

*The only freedom that is of enduring importance is
the freedom of intelligence, that is to say, freedom of
observation and of judgment.*

JOHN DEWEY

Michael Chang[1] began his career in a small consulting company. As a young manager, he was forceful with his opinion and erred toward brutal honesty. Over time, he saw its damaging effects and reflected, "It certainly doesn't get people to blossom."

As Michael gained leadership experience, he began to realize that when you become the leader, the center of gravity is no longer yourself. He had a mentor who taught him that the leader's job is to put other people on stage. He began to shift his focus to others, and he became less controlling and learned to give people space. Where he used to jump in and do it for them, he learned to hold back. He found that not only do other people step up, they often surprise you by producing something better than you would have. As he has grown as a leader, he's learned to be direct without being destructive. He's learned how to create an environment where he could tell the truth and have others grow from it.

Today, this manager is the CEO of a thriving start-up company. He has developed several practices that give space for others to do their best work. He makes a conscious effort to create a learning environment by recruiting people with a strong learning orientation and then often admitting his own mistakes. This gives others permission to make and recover from their own mistakes. When offering his opinion, he distinguishes "hard opinions" from "soft opinions." Soft opinions signal to his team: *here are some ideas for you to consider in your own thinking.* Hard opinions are reserved for times when he holds a very strong view.

Here's a leader who began his career headed down the path of a management tyrant but who has become a Multiplier and Liberator himself. The accomplishment is significant when you consider the path of least resistance for most smart, driven leaders is to become a Tyrant. Even Michael said, "It's not like it isn't temping to be tyrannical when you can."

Let's face it. Corporate environments and modern organizations are the perfect setup for diminishing leadership and have a certain built-in tyranny. The org charts, the hierarchy, the titles, the approval matrixes skew power toward the top and create incentives for people to shut down and comply. In any hierarchical organization, the playing field is rarely level. The senior leaders stand on the high side of the field and ideas and policies roll easily down to the lower side. Policies— established to create order—often unintentionally keep people from thinking. At best, these policies limit intellectual range of motion as they straitjacket the thinking of the followers. At worst, these systems shut down thinking entirely.

These hierarchical structures make it easy for Tyrants to reign. And in their reign, these managers can easily suppress and constrain the thinking of the people around them.

Consider the fate of Kate, a corporate manager who began her career as an intelligent, driven, and creative collaborator. She was promoted into management and moved quickly from front-line manager to vice president and is now running a large organization. She still sees herself as an open-minded, creative thought leader. But in a recent 360 degree feedback report, she was shocked to find that her people don't seem to agree. As she read the report, she could see that her strong ideas were hampering the creativity and capability of her people. And her drive for results was making it difficult for people to be truthful and take risks. One of the comments read, "It is just easier to hold back and let Kate do the thinking." Kate was stunned.

Every step she had taken up the corporate ladder made it that much easier for her to unintentionally kill other people's ideas. The nature of the hierarchy had skewed power, making every conversation Kate had with a subordinate inherently unequal. The playing field was tilted in her favor. An off-the-cuff remark could be translated as a strong opinion and turned into policy for her division. If she rolled her eyes or sighed sharply after someone's comment, everyone in the room noticed and avoided saying anything they thought would produce the same reaction. She had more power than she had realized. She had become an Accidental Diminisher.

I suspect I saw too many military movies in college because they all started to look alike. Inevitably there would be a scene where an army private who was privy to some debacle would stand at attention and nervously appeal to the commanding officer, "Permission to speak freely, sir?" I could never understand this strange custom and why someone would need permission to speak freely. After all, I was in college where thinking and speaking freely was the norm. However, after several years in the workplace, I clearly understood. Formal hierarchies suppressed the voices, and often ideas, of those at the bottom.

Multipliers liberate people from the oppressive forces within corporate hierarchy. They liberate people to think, to speak, and to act with reason. They create an environment where the best ideas surface and where people do their best work. They give people permission to think.

THE TYRANT VERSUS THE LIBERATOR

Multipliers create an intense environment in which superior thinking and work can flourish. Tyrants create a tense environment that suppresses people's thinking and capability.

A Tense Leader

Jenna Healy was an SVP of field operations for a large telecommunications company. She was a serious leader who even at five feet, three inches had a way of towering over the people who worked for her. Jenna was a smart manager with strong experience, but Jenna was an absolute Tyrant.

Her colleagues said, "She created an environment of hysteria. She created fear all around her and intimidated and bullied people until she got what she wanted. Her primary approach to leadership was 'What more can you do for me?'" When one of her managers said, "She's a bit like the ruthless Miranda Priestly in *The Devil Wears Prada*," I got the picture immediately.

Not only was Jenna a bully, but she struck at random. It was hard to predict what would set her off or who would be the next victim. One person recalled, "You felt like you could be the next guy. I was stressed, on the edge, and at risk around her." Her colleagues joked, "There needs to be a storm warning system for Jenna. People need to know when it is time to duck and cover."

Jenna's quarterly management meeting in Denver was one such time. Jenna had gathered a cross-functional team to review the state of the business in the U.S. market. It was a typical business review with each function, in turn, presenting its "state of the business." After several presentations, Daniel, the manager of the information technology team, began his presentation by showing the managers the data for how their field service staff was utilizing the IT tools that his team had built for them. He then inquired, "In light of these numbers, I wonder if the service teams are taking advantage of the tools that already exist?" Based on Jenna's reaction, you would have thought he had just told her that her team was stupid and lazy. She snapped, "You have no idea what you are talking about," and then berated him in front of the group. The argument got heated and lasted for an uncomfortable ten minutes. When somebody finally signaled that the group was overdue for a break, there was a rapid dash for the conference room door. But Daniel stayed in an attempt to hold his ground against Jenna. With everyone out in the hall, the argument escalated irrationally and turned to shouting.

While things were heated in the conference room, outside in the hall there was a distinct chill in the air. Everyone in the hall was quietly cheering Daniel for standing up to the bully, but those who were next up to present were frozen with fear. You could feel the tension. The fortunate ones who had already given their presentations wished luck to their ill-fated colleagues. These remaining presenters began scrambling to adjust their presentations, taking out anything controversial that might incite the already livid leader. The presenters watered down their presentations, and they got through the meeting, but nothing much was really said and nothing much was accomplished.

Jenna's organization made some modest progress but continually failed to hit its revenue and service quality targets. Eventually, when she went too far and bullied one of their partners, she was exited instantly from the organization. Jenna went to another company as COO. She lasted two weeks before being demoted. Six months later she was asked to leave.

People hold back around leaders like Jenna. Such Tyrants shut down the flow of intelligence and rarely access people's best work. Everywhere they go, they find people doing less than they really can. It is no wonder they resort to intimidation, thinking it will get them what they no doubt want—great thinking and great work. But intimidation and fear rarely produce truly great work.

Let's look at another senior sales and services leader.

An Intense Leader

Robert Enslin is the president of SAP North America, the global software giant. Originally from South Africa, he speaks with a calm confidence. Robert is highly respected with a reputation as a fair, consistent sales leader who grows organizations and delivers results.

Robert operates as a peer to everyone he works with and is accessible to all. One of his managers said of him, "He is very good at disarming you. He is a commoner—one of us. Even if you work three levels below him, he still wants to know what you think." As a result, people are more transparent around him. They don't feel like they have to tell him what he wants to hear. This approachability creates safety for the people around Robert. And that safety is what allows him to run a massive sales organization with no surprises.

Several years ago, Robert was asked to take over the Japanese subsidiary for SAP to address some very specific sales performance issues. When he met with his new leadership team in Japan for the first forecast meeting, he could see the forecasting process was in complete disarray. Instead of playing the authoritarian, judging their failure and dictating his solution, Robert restrained himself and started a learning process. He helped them realize the limitations of the current process and the advantages of a new approach. He then drew on their knowledge of the Japanese business and asked them, "How can we take this to the next level?" He created space for the team to try new approaches and fix the problem themselves. He stayed with them on the issue for months until they could run a forecast process that delivered solid, predictable results for the business.

Robert was known for his collegial approach and his calm consistency, but this was tested when he took over the North American business in 2008, just as the global economy was melting down. As spending was locking up and large capital purchases were being put on hold, executives everywhere were beginning to panic. You could feel the tension as you walked through the halls of SAP's Newtown

Square office near Philadelphia. One step past the glass door, you could feel the tension as you entered the executive conference room.

Inside another conference room, Robert and his new management team were assembled to plan their sales strategy in this new economic environment. Every person on his team knew that Robert had been meeting with the senior executives and was under a lot of pressure. They came to the meeting prepared to feel their share of the pain—after all, this was a sales organization. But Robert was calm and constant, even amid this chaos. His team began to wonder if he hadn't been reading the news or had skipped the executive meetings. He opened the meeting by acknowledging the severity of the economic issues, but suggested they put them aside. He kept the team focused on the issues within their control. He then asked, "What can we do to differentiate ourselves right now?" Safe within their sphere of expertise and control, the group worked to identify the value proposition that would help them position their solutions in the turbulent climate. After the discussion, he then asked, "How can we help people consume our products so they get the most economic value?" Again, the group could wrestle this question down and put together a plan.

His team said, "We know he must have been getting pressure from up higher, but he didn't create anxiety for us. He remained calm and just never wigged out. He doesn't create whiplash for his people."

Robert's calmness is not synonymous with softness. He is as intense and focused as any other successful sales executive. The difference is where his focus lies. A member of his leadership team said, "With Robert, it isn't about him. He makes it about you and about getting the best work from you."

Robert's steady hand and open environment provide sanity and stability to an organization that could have easily spun into crisis.

Tense Versus Intense

Tyrants create a *tense* environment—one that is full of stress and anxiety. Liberators like Robert create an *intense* environment that requires concentration, diligence, and energy. It is an environment where people are encouraged to think for themselves but also where people experience a deep obligation to do their best work.

Diminishers create a stress-filled environment because they don't give people control over their own performance. They operate as Tyrants, overexerting their will on the organization. They cause others to shrink, retreat, and hold back. In the presence of a Tyrant, people try not to stand out. Just consider how people operate under the rule of a political dictator. Tyrants get diminished thinking from others because people only offer the safest of ideas and mediocre work.

While a Tyrant creates stress that causes people to hold back, a Liberator creates space for people to step up. While a Tyrant swings between positions that create whiplash in the organization, a Liberator builds stability that generates forward momentum.

THE LIBERATOR

The Liberator creates an environment where good things happen. They create the conditions where intelligence is engaged, grown, and transformed into concrete successes. What are the conditions for this cycle of learning and success? They might include:

- Ideas are generated with ease.

- People learn rapidly and adapt to new environments.

- People work collaboratively.

- Complex problems get solved.

- Difficult tasks get accomplished.

Let's examine three Liberators from very different industries who created these conditions and freed their organizations to think and to perform.

Liberator #1: Equity in the Firm

Ernest Bachrach from Argentina is the managing partner and co-head of Latin America for Advent International, a global private equity firm. With twenty-seven years of experience in international private equity and an MBA from Harvard University, Ernest is clearly an expert. But the source of his genius is the environment he creates to unleash the genius of his organization.

One of his analysts described his approach: "Ernest makes a conscious effort to create an environment. He creates forums for people to voice their ideas. But he holds a very high bar for what you must do before you voice an opinion. You need to have the data. He has a problem with opinions without data."

Ernest builds a learning machine in his organization. When he discovers performance problems, he is quick to give feedback. The feedback is direct and sometimes harsh, but he dispenses the feedback in small enough doses that someone can absorb it, learn from it and adjust. He teaches his organization that mistakes are a way of life in the investment business. And how does he respond to mistakes? First, he doesn't panic or assign arbitrary blame. One team member said, "He lets us know that when decisions are collective, the mistakes are collective, too. No one person takes the blame." The team then does a postmortem and learns how to avoid the error a second time.

It appears that Ernest understands how to create an environment that best leverages the investments he has made in his people. This might be one factor in his recent promotion to chief executive of Advent in Latin America.

Liberator #2: Close Encounters

Everyone knows Steven Spielberg as an award-winning film director. It is likely that your top-ten movie list includes one of his films. But why are his movies so successful, grossing an average of $156 million per film? Some would posit that it is his creative genius and his ability to tell a story. Others would point to his work ethic. But the active agent may be his ability to elicit more from his crew than other directors do. People who have worked on Spielberg's films say, "You do your best work around him."

One way he elicits the best thinking from people is that he knows what people are actually capable of producing. He knows everyone's job intimately, but he doesn't do it for them. He tells them that he has hired them because he admires their work. He uses his knowledge of the job and of their personal capabilities to set a standard for demanding their best work.

He comes with strong ideas of his own, but he makes it clear that bad ideas are an okay starting point. He says, "All good ideas start as bad ideas. That's why it takes so long." He establishes an open, creative environment, but he still demands extraordinary work from his team. One of his crew members said, "He expects people to be doing their best. And you know it when you aren't giving your best."

And why does Spielberg produce so many successful movies? Because his crew is twice as productive as those of some of the Tyrant directors we studied. Because Spielberg creates an environment where people can do their best work, these artists and staff sign up to work with him again and again. In fact, Spielberg typically manages two projects simultaneously, each in different production stages, because his crew stays with him and rolls directly onto the next project. He gets their best work and 2X the productivity! And they get to create award-winning films along with him.

Liberator #3: A Master Teacher

Stop and think about the best teachers you've had. Pause for a moment and identify one or two in your mind. What type of learning environment did they create? How much space and freedom of thought did you have? What were the expectations of your performance? In what ways were you stretched and utilized? And how did you actually perform? I asked these questions of a dozen eighth-grade students in Mr. Kelly's class.

Patrick Kelly is an eighth-grade U.S. history and social studies teacher at a distinguished California public school. He caught my attention when I learned that every year at middle school graduation ceremony, he not only gets more "shout-outs and thank-yous" from the graduating students than any other teacher, he gets more than all the other teachers combined. He is more talked about, more loathed, more beloved than any other teacher at the school. Why?

I got my first glimpse at the fall parent information night at La Entrada Middle School. It is one of those nights parents with multiple children dread because, with four children, I have to get to seventeen different teachers' classes, many simultaneously, defying laws of physics. My daughter in eighth grade said to me, "Here's my class schedule. Get to as many classes as you can, but be sure to make it to Mr. Kelly's social studies class. And do *not* be late. And do not talk during his presentation. And do not answer your cell phone. And do *not* be late. Mom, did you hear me about not being late?" I entered his classroom both scared and intrigued. After the standard twelve-minute segment with Mr. Kelly, I left enchanted with eighth-grade social studies, ready to quit my job and go back to middle school to learn U.S. history.

Why does he affect students and parents alike in such powerful ways?

It begins with his classroom environment. He makes it clear that you are there to work hard, to think, and to learn. One student said, "In his class, he doesn't tolerate laziness. You're always working, thinking things over, and seeing your mistakes so you can learn from them." It's a professional and serious environment, which gets lighter and more fun as the students work harder. In this environment, students are encouraged to speak up and voice their opinions. Equal weight is given to asking a good question as answering one of his.

Mr. Kelly's expectations for the students' learning are both clear and extremely high. One student said, "He believes that with high expectations come high results. He demands our best. He makes it clear that if we put in our hardest effort, we will succeed." Another said, "He doesn't hide anything from us and lets us know what to improve on. He demands that we work to the best of our ability." No more, no less—just to the best of their ability. There is no homework in his class—nothing assigned, nothing arbitrary. Instead, students are encouraged to do "independent study" to help them understand the ideas and perform well on tests. The students, having made the choice themselves, do the independent study with zeal.

Not all students like Mr. Kelly. Some find him too tough, too demanding, and his expectations unfair compared to other teachers'. For students wanting the easy path, his class can be an uncomfortable environment. But most students are engaged by his intelligence and his dedication and thrive under his leadership. They experience his contagious passion and themselves become passionate about civil rights, the U.S. Constitution, and their role in the political process.

Patrick Kelly is a Multiplier who liberates his students to think and learn. He creates an environment where students can speak out but where they are required to think and perform at their finest. It won't surprise you that 98 percent of students in his class score at the "proficient" or "advanced" levels on standardized state tests, up from 82 percent just three years ago.[2]

A Hybrid Climate

The secret behind the environment in Mr. Kelly's classroom (and Ernest Bachrach's firm and Steven Spielberg's movie sets) is in a duality we consistently found with Liberators. They appear to hold two ostensibly opposing positions with equal fervor. They create both comfort *and* pressure in the environment. In the eyes of the Liberator, it is a just exchange: I give you space; you give me back your best work.

Liberators also give people space to make mistakes. They create an environment of learning, but they expect people to learn from the mistakes. It is another fair trade: I give you permission to make mistakes; you have an obligation to learn from the mistakes and not repeat them.

The power of Liberators emanates from this duality. It isn't enough to just free people's thinking. They create an intense environment that requires people's best thinking *and* their best work. They generate pressure, but they don't generate stress.

Liberators operate with a duality much like that of a hybrid car that switches over seamlessly between the electric and the gasoline engine. At low speeds, a hybrid operates in electric mode. At high speeds, it draws on the gasoline to fuel the extra demands on the engine. Such leaders create an open, comfortable environment where people can freely think and contribute. But when more power is needed, they invoke their demanding side that commands only the best performance from others.

How do Liberators create a safe, open environment, but also relentlessly demand the best thinking and work of those around them? How do they get the full brainpower of the organization? Let's turn to the practices of the Liberator for answers.

THE THREE PRACTICES OF THE LIBERATOR

Among the Multipliers we studied in our research, we found three common practices. Liberators: 1) create space; 2) demand people's best work; and 3) generate rapid learning cycles. We'll examine each in turn.

I. Create Space

Everyone needs space. We need space to contribute and to work. Liberators don't take it for granted that people have the space they need. They deliberately carve out space for others to be able to make a contribution. They do so in the following ways.

Release Others by Restraining Yourself

It is a small victory to create space for others to contribute. But it is a huge victory to maintain that space and resist the temptation to jump back in and consume it yourself. This is especially true in formal, hierarchical organizations where people are accustomed to deferring to their leaders.

Ray Lane, former president of Oracle Corporation and current managing partner at Kleiner Perkins venture capital, is a master at executive restraint. One of his portfolio CEOs remarked, "Ray has learned the importance of restraint in leadership. He knows that less is more, and he never wastes an opinion."

When Ray goes on sales calls to meet with executives at a potential client's, two things are certain: 1) The client will want to hear from Ray and his vast experience and 2) Ray will be prepared. But despite these forces pulling him in, he holds back. He makes a few opening pleasantries, but he lets the sales team do the deal. Issues come up in conversation that Ray has a point of view about, but still he waits. The sales team, knowing full well that Ray could probably be doing a better job than they, continues their work nonetheless. When they are done, Ray then comes into the conversation. He still doesn't unleash his ideas and give a monologue. He has listened carefully and knows exactly what he wants to add. He dispenses his views in small but intense doses.

A longtime colleague of Ray remarked, "He'll often be quiet for long stretches of an important meeting. He listens to what others are saying. And when he does speak, everyone listens."

Ray is well known as a brilliant strategist and perhaps one of the most articulate communicators in his business. But instead of overplaying himself and his own ideas, he creates room for others and uses his presence where it can have the greatest potency and impact for the team.

Shift the Ratio of Listening to Talking

Liberators are more than just good listeners. They are ferocious listeners. They listen to feed their hunger for knowledge. They listen to learn what other people know and add it to their own reservoir of knowledge. As management guru C.K. Prahalad said to me, "How smart you are is defined by how clearly you can see the intellect of others." They listen intently because they are trying to learn and understand what other people know.

John Brandon, one of Apple Inc.'s top sales executives, runs an organization that brings in over $12 billion in revenue each year across three regions of the world. John is a high-energy sales leader and maintains an aggressive travel and meeting schedule, so getting time on his calendar can be tough. But when his direct reports meet with him one-on-one, they get his whole presence. John listens intently to them and is keenly interested in understanding their reality—what is really happening on the ground, with customers and with deals. He asks probing questions that get to the heart of the matter. One of his direct reports said, "The difference with John is not that he listens; it is that he listens to an extreme." In a typical conversation, he spends 80 percent of the time listening and asking questions. By listening, asking, and probing, John develops an understanding of the realities of the business and an understanding with his team of the opportunities and problems they face. This collective insight into the market has enabled John's organization to experience a phenomenal 375 percent growth over the last five years. John, who can certainly talk a good game himself, knows when it is time to listen.

Liberators don't just listen the majority of time. They massively shift the ratio, listening most of the time. This creates space for others to share what they know.

Operate Consistently

Imagine a troop of young girls competing in double-dutch jump rope. Visualize the smooth, even rhythm of the turning ropes. The turners stand at the ropes' ends and rapidly turn the two ropes in opposite directions. Their role is clear and vital—maintain both a consistent arc and a constant speed. Their consistency is what makes it safe for the jumpers to enter the whirling space. Any erratic turns or inconsistency and a jumper can't enter or trips doing so. Consistency creates predictability. When leaders are consistent, it lets others know when they can jump in and allows them to contribute.

Operating with consistency is one of the most vital of the practices of the Liberator. In our interviews, we continually heard how Multipliers operate with a consistency that enables others. For example, John Brandon was described as "comfortable, consistent, confident, relaxed, and disarming." Craig Conway, former CEO of PeopleSoft, "took emotion out of every situation. He put a consistently professional front to everything."

The consistency of their actions creates two effects: 1) It establishes a predictable pattern of behavior. This allows others to know when it is their turn and where there is space for them to contribute. 2) It creates safety. When people operate in predictable ways, we know what to expect and we become comfortable around them. This comfort allows people not only to jump in, but to do so with full power of thought.

Recall how Robert Enslin's consistent leadership created a calming effect on his organization. He was able to contain stress instead of flowing it out to the organization. This consistency gave people the platform for transparency and the ability to focus on the real issues—delivering value to SAP customers, which, in turn, delivered revenue to the corporation.

Level the Playing Field

In any formal organization, the playing field is rarely level, and certain voices are inherently advantaged. These include senior executives, influential thought leaders, critical organizations like product development or sales, and people with deep legacy knowledge. Unless managed, other voices that are perhaps closest to the real issues can become muffled. Liberators amplify these voices to extract maximum intelligence and give advantage to the ideas and voices on the lower end of the playing field.

When Nick Reilly—the first president and CEO of GM Daewoo Auto and Technology (GMDAT)—took the reins, he brought together the American automaker and a very traditional Korean company. He also took explicit steps to level the playing field. Reilly created a senior leadership team consisting of four Koreans, three Europeans, and four Americans. Reilly, a native of the U.K., knew the GM team was likely to dominate. Yet it was clear to him that the success of the operation depended on the team's ability to draw on the talent and intellectual assets of the former Daewoo members.

Reilly served as an amplifier, establishing systems for drawing out the contributions of the Korean team members, who were all in their midfifties and initially spoke limited English. He made sure that all executive meetings were simultaneously translated into Korean. At every turn, he showed respect for the Korean team and the legacy Daewoo had built. He asked the Korean team members what aspects of Daewoo's culture needed to be preserved, and consequently protected them. He created learning teams by pairing Koreans and non-Koreans to work together and learn from each other. Out of these two cultures, he created a third joint culture based on a set of common values and a level playing field. The team created a new mission, vision, and values for the organization and began to embed them in the Korean operations.

Under Reilly's leadership, functional silos were reduced and a company that had been on the brink of liquidation became a major revenue source for General Motors. It also became a hub for global small car design and development, with complete vehicles and kits for assembly at other GM facilities being sold in more than 150 countries worldwide (a 3,000 percent volume increase in one year alone!). One senior executive stated, "The way Nick led this joint venture created a higher level of aspiration for all of us."

GMDAT is not exempt from the challenges of today's business world and has recently posted a loss, but in October 2009, GM increased its ownership stake in GMDAT to 70.1 percent—a strong statement of its belief in its Korean unit. Reilly now heads GM International Operations and, in October 2009, was named an honorary citizen of Seoul.

Liberators begin by creating space, but they do more than create space for others to contribute. Yes, they do provide the space, but they also expect extraordinary work in return.

II. Demand People's Best Work

Henry Kissinger, Secretary of State under Richard Nixon, was a master at getting people's best work. According to one story, his chief of staff once handed in a report he had written on an aspect of foreign policy. When Kissinger received the report, he asked simply, "Is this your best work?" The chief thought for a moment and, worried that his boss would think the report was not good enough, responded, "Mr. Kissinger, I think I can do better." So Kissinger gave the report back. Two weeks later the chief turned in the revised report. Kissinger kept it for a week and then sent it back with a note that said, "Are you sure this is your best work?" Realizing that something must have been missing, the chief once again rewrote the report. This time when he handed the report to his boss he said, "Mr. Kissinger, this is my best work." Upon hearing this, Kissinger replied, "Then this time I will read your report."[3]

Here are a few ways that Liberators demand the best from those they work with.

Defend the Standard

Larry Gelwix, the head coach of Highland Rugby, stood at the center of a huddle of rugby players at the side of the field for the team's first game debrief of the season. Larry asked one question, "Did you give your *best*?"

One player enthusiastically spoke up, "Well we won, didn't we?" Not unkindly, Larry said, "That's not the question I asked." Another player jumped in. "We just dominated that team. We won 64 to 20. What more could you ask for?" Larry said, "When you came for tryouts, I said I expected your *best*. That means your best thinking out there as well as your best physical effort. Is that what you gave today?"

One player described one game played on the island of Tonga when he could answer "yes" to Larry's question. He said, "I had a painful shoulder contusion after a devastating tackle on my opponent. I was ready to quit, ready to let my team down. I couldn't lift my arm and the pain was excruciating. I remember I began to chant the *haka* [a traditional Maori war chant] in my head. I remember looking over at the sunset through the palm trees. At that very moment the game seemed to stop, and I had a choice. A voice told me that I needed to keep going and do my best, not only for myself, but for who I am, and most importantly for the team—for my brothers. The voice was the recollection of countless practices and games when Coach Gelwix simply asked, 'Is that your best?' I finished that game with two tries [each the equivalent of a touchdown] becoming the first high school American to score in Tonga."

As a manager you know when someone is below his or her usual performance. What is harder to know is whether people are giving everything they have to give. Asking whether people are giving their best gives them the opportunity to push themselves beyond their previous limits. It is a key reason why people report that Multipliers get more than 100 percent intelligence out of them.

Distinguish Best Work from Outcomes

Requiring people's best work is different from insisting on desired outcomes. Stress is created when people are expected to produce outcomes that are beyond their control. But they feel positive pressure when they are held to their best work.

K.R. Sridhar, CEO of Bloom Energy, innovator of green-power generators globally, and a renowned scientist himself, has mastered this distinction in his company. He said, "If you want your organization to take risks, you have to separate the experiment from the outcome. I have zero tolerance if someone does not run the experiment. But I don't hold them accountable for the outcome of the experiment. I only hold them accountable to execute." This is one of Bloom Energy's secrets for innovating across complex, integrated technologies.

K.R. understands the distinction between pressure and stress. He cites the famous image of William Tell shooting an apple off his son's head: "In this scenario, William Tell feels pressure. His son feels stress." K.R. keeps the pressure on his team to act, but doesn't create stress by holding them accountable for outcomes beyond their control.

III. Generate Rapid Learning Cycles

In studying Multipliers, I have often wondered, *How smart do you have to be to be a Multiplier?* The answer from Bill Campbell, chairman and former CEO of Intuit was perfect: "You have to be smart enough to learn."

Perhaps most important, Liberators give people permission to make mistakes and the obligation to learn from them.

Admit and Share Mistakes

When Lutz Ziob took over as general manager of the education business at Microsoft in 2003, it was falling short of its goals for revenue and reach. Lutz needed to make progress fast and could have easily created a stressful environment around him. But he also needed the organization to be creative and take risks if they were to catch up in the market. It was a classic management dilemma. If you take the obvious path, the climate will become tense and your people may become risk averse. However, if you lessen the pressure by softening the goals, then your organization becomes complacent. Lutz did neither.

Instead, he created an environment that was equal parts pressure and learning. Lutz never backed down from the natural pressure for the business to perform, but he made it safe for people to take risks and make mistakes. He did this by how he responded to both his mistakes and the mistakes of others.

Lutz was shameless in speaking about his own mistakes. He loves to tell stories, and his favorites are about his mistakes. Instead of hiding his own mistakes or diffusing them onto his staff, he confesses them. When he launched an unsuccessful product, he talked about it openly and what he learned from it. One member of his management team said, "He brings an intellectual curiosity for why things didn't work out." By taking his mistakes public, he made it safe for others to take risks and fail.

Insist on Learning from Mistakes

Lutz creates room for other people to make mistakes. When Chris Pirie, the general manager for sales and marketing working for Lutz, was newly promoted to lead sales for Microsoft Learning, he tried a risky promotion. Unfortunately it didn't work. But instead of rationalizing the mistake, he went to Lutz and admitted the misstep, diagnosed it, and then tried something different. Chris said, "With Lutz, you get to make mistakes. But you are expected to learn fast. With Lutz, it's okay to fail. You just can't make the same mistake twice."

Lutz loves feedback. He isn't just open to it. He insists on it. A direct report of his recalled a time he had to give Lutz some tough-love feedback. Lutz was involved in a critical project and was particularly excited about the possibilities for the business. As such, he had been dominating the discussion and had taken over. Lutz's direct report scheduled a one-on-one. He sat down in Lutz's office and delivered the feedback: "Lutz, you are sucking the oxygen out of the room. No one else has any room to breathe. You need to back off." How do you think Lutz responded? How would you have responded if one of your people suggested you were a domineering oxygen hog? Lutz's curiosity was triggered, and his response was simple. He asked, "What does it look like? Who did it impact? How do I avoid doing it again?" After taking the time to understand his mistake, he asked his direct report, "Will you tell me if I do this again?" His final comment to his direct report was, "I wish you would have told me sooner." He really meant it.

Lutz achieved the climate he wanted even amidst a stressful external environment by generating rapid learning cycles. As Chris Pirie said, "Lutz creates an environment where good things happen." Even in times of immense external pressure, Lutz created a climate that drew out people's best thinking and work. He maintained a creative intensity.

Tyrants and Liberators both expect mistakes. Tyrants stand ready to pounce on the people who make them. Liberators stand ready to learn as much from the mistake as possible. The highest quality of thinking cannot emerge without learning. Learning can't happen without mistakes. Liberators get the best thinking from people by creating a rapid cycle between thinking, learning, and making and recovering from mistakes. They move rapidly through this cycle in order to generate the best ideas and create an agile organization. As K.R. Sridhar explained, "We iterate fast so we can bring cycle time down. The key to this rapid iteration is creating an environment where people can bring up risks and deal with mistakes sooner." A.G. Lafley, former CEO at Procter & Gamble said, "You want your people to fail early, fast, and cheap—and then learn from it."

Diminishers don't generate these cycles. They might request—if not demand—people's best thinking, but they fail to establish the environment where ideas are easily expressed and developed to full maturity and efficacy.

THE DIMINISHER'S APPROACH TO ENVIRONMENT

Diminishers haven't developed this smooth duality of comfort and pressure. Instead, they jerk the organization around as they swing between two modes: 1) militant insistence on their ideas and 2) passive indifference to the ideas and work of others.

Timothy Wilson is an award-winning Hollywood property master. He and his team set the scene and create context for a movie, and he has worked on some of the biggest and most successful films. He's a creative genius, but he comes at a high cost. Why? Because so few people are willing to work with him *twice*.

One of his staff said, "I'd take any job before working with him." Signing up to work with Timothy means working in fear and stress with little enjoyment. Those who do work for him say, "You don't want to come back to work the next day." From the moment Timothy steps onto the set, the mood changes. People brace for his criticism. As Jeremy sees Timothy walk over to one of the props that he had been working on for the last two days, Jeremy wonders which of the usual insults it will be. Or will he perhaps deliver a rare compliment? Timothy inspects the prop, and delivers his signature critique, loudly and to the whole group, "This looks like a prop for a B movie." And then there are the random things that set him off. If the prop cart isn't organized correctly, he goes crazy. One day he got so tense that he argued with the director of photography and threw his walkie-talkie at him. The set went from tense to tenser as people prepared to duck and cover.

Some leaders create an *intense* environment that requires people's best thinking and work. Timothy created a *tense* environment by dominating the space, creating anxiety, and judging others in a way that had a stifling effect on people's thinking and output.

DOMINATE THE SPACE. Tyrants are like a gas that expands and consumes all the available space. They dominate meetings and hog all the air time. They leave little room for anyone else and often suffocate other people's intelligence in the process. They do this by voicing strong opinions, overexpressing their ideas and trying to maintain control. Garth Yamamoto, chief marketing officer at a consumer products company, uses up almost every cubic inch of space in the room. He jumps in and interrupts people's presentations, he expresses very strong and extreme opinions, and either spends his time micromanaging or is noticeably absent. People warn newcomers in his division, "The art of being successful around here is figuring out Garth." One member of his group said, "I think I am atrophying here. I'm probably giving him about 50 percent." That person has since left the organization and is thriving in another company.

CREATE ANXIETY. The hallmark of a Tyrant is their temperamental and unpredictable behavior. People don't know what will set them off, but it is almost certain that the mood will change when they are around. It is as if Tyrants impose an "anxiety tax" wherever they go. A percentage of people's mental energy is consumed trying to avoid upsetting the Tyrant. Just think of the wasted productivity on the set with Timothy Wilson. Instead of using their full energy making "A movie" props, Timothy's team worries about the next thing that Timothy is going to say or do or, for that matter, throw.

JUDGE OTHERS. Tyrants centralize their power and play judge, jury, and executioner. In sharp contrast to the rapid learning cycles of the Liberator, Tyrants create cycles of criticism, judgment, and retreat. Like the presenters scurrying to adjust their presentations for Jenna Healy (the telecommunications sales leader who resembled Miranda Priestly in *The Devil Wears Prada*), people retreat to a safe position where their ideas won't be criticized or exposed. The Japanese have a saying for this: *Deru kui wa utareru*, which translated means, "The stake that sticks out gets hammered down."

When leaders play the role of the Tyrant, they suppress people's thinking and capability. People restrain themselves and work cautiously, only bringing up safe ideas that the leader is likely to agree with. This is why Diminishers are costly to organizations. Under the influence of a Diminisher, the organization pays full price for a resource but only receives about 50 percent of its value.

FROM LIBERATION TO RESOURCE LEVERAGE

Why do Liberators get the full value from their resources?

Multipliers know that people are intelligent and will figure it out. Because they engage people's natural intelligence, people offer them back their full brainpower. Because people have a foundation of safety and comfort, they are free to offer their boldest ideas, not just the safe ideas that will keep them out of the wrath of a Tyrant. The environment of learning has enabled them to take risks, and quickly and inexpensively recover from them.

There is an assumption that underlies the practices of a Liberator. It is that *people's best thinking must be given, not taken*. A manager may be able to insist on certain levels of productivity and output, but someone's full effort, including their truly discretionary effort, must be given voluntarily. This changes the leader's role profoundly. Instead of demanding the best work directly, they create an environment where it not only can be offered, but where it is deeply needed. Because the environment naturally requires it, a person freely bestows their best thinking and work.

Multipliers not only get full brainpower from their team, they grow capability rapidly. Our research shows that they don't just get twice more, they get twice the capability with an extra 5 to 10 percent growth bonus.

Diminishers, on the other hand, believe that *pressure increases performance*. They demand people's best thinking, but they don't get it. They fail to establish the environment where ideas are easily expressed and developed to full maturity and efficacy. An unsafe environment yields only the safest ideas.

The following chart reflects why Tyrants leave capability on the table while Liberators extract full intelligence and capability from the people around them.

Tyrants		Liberators	
What They Do	*What They Get*	*What They Do*	*What They Get*
Create a tense environment that suppresses people's thinking and capability	People who hold back but appear to be engaged on the surface Safe ideas the leader already agrees with People who work cautiously, avoid taking risks, and find excuses for any mistakes they make	Create an intense environment that requires people's best thinking and work	People who offer their best thinking and really engage their full brainpower The best and boldest ideas People who give their full effort and will go out on a limb and learn quickly from any mistakes

The promise of a Multiplier is twice the capacity. Let's now look at a few of the starting points for how someone becomes a Liberator to their organization.

BECOMING A LIBERATOR

Remember that the path of least resistance is often the path of the Diminisher. As Michael said, "It's not like it isn't tempting to be tyrannical when you can." Becoming a Liberator requires long-term commitment. Here are a few starting points.

The Starting Block

1. PLAY YOUR CHIPS. If you want to create more room for others to contribute, and especially if you are prone to dominating a discussion, you might consider a good game of poker chips.

Matthew is a smart, articulate leader. However, he often found himself frustrated and out ahead of his organization, struggling to bring a cross-functional team along with him and his ideas. He was also struggling to be heard. He had great ideas, but he was simply talking too much and taking up too much space in team meetings. I was working with him to prepare a critical leadership forum for his division. He was eagerly awaiting the opportunity to share his views about the strategy for advancing the business to the next level. Instead of encouraging him, I gave him a challenge.

I gave him five poker chips, each worth a number of seconds of talk time. One was worth 120 seconds, the next three worth 90 seconds, and one was worth just 30. I suggested he limit his contribution in the meeting to five comments, represented by each of the chips. He could spend them whenever he wished, but he only had five. After the initial shock and bemusement (wondering how he could possibly convey all his ideas in five comments), he accepted the challenge. I watched as he carefully restrained himself, filtering his thoughts for only the most essential and looking for the right moment to insert his ideas. He played his poker chips deftly and achieved two important outcomes: 1) he created abundant space for others. Instead of it being Matthew's strategy session, it became a forum for a diverse group to voice ideas and co-create the strategy, and 2) Matthew increased his own credibility and presence as a leader. By exercising some leadership restraint, everyone was heard more, including Matthew as the leader.

Try giving yourself a budget of poker chips for a meeting. Maybe it is five; maybe it is just one or two. Use them wisely, and leave the rest of the space for others to contribute.

2. LABEL YOUR OPINIONS. As you know, formal organizations can create a strong deference to the opinions and thinking of the leader. One executive described his first week as the newly appointed president of a large company. People came at him from all directions to ask him their pent-up questions. He was new and wanted to be helpful, so he would offer a casual opinion. To his amazement, weeks later he found that his opinions had become a set of disjointed policies. As he unraveled the mess, he learned to carefully label the difference between a random musing, an opinion, and a policy decision.

Try the practice used by Michael Chang, in his shift to Liberator. Divide your views into "soft opinions" and "hard opinions":

- *Soft opinions:* where you have a perspective to offer and ideas for someone else to consider

- *Hard opinions:* where you have a clear and potentially emphatic point of view

By doing so, you can create space for others to comfortably disagree with your "soft opinion" thinking and establish their own views. Reserve the right to have "hard opinions" for when it really matters.

3. MAKE YOUR MISTAKES KNOWN. There is no easier way to invite experimentation and learning than to share stories about your own mistakes. As a leader, your acknowledgment of your personal mistakes will give others permission to experience failure and go on to learn and recover with dignity and increased capability.

Great parents do this with their children. They understand that their children are liberated when they know their parents are human and make mistakes just as they do. They especially appreciate knowing that their parents learned from their blunders and recovered. When we help people see a path to recovery, we spawn a learning cycle.

As you share your mistakes, try these two approaches:

1. *Get personal:* Let people know mistakes you have made and what you have learned from them. Let them know how you have incorporated this learning into your decisions and current leadership practices. As a manager of a consulting group, you might share with your team the time you led a project that failed and how you dealt with the livid customer. You can focus on what the experience taught you and how it shaped your current approach to project management.

2. *Go public:* Instead of talking about mistakes behind closed doors or just one-on-one, bring them out in the open where the person making a mistake can clear the air and where everyone can learn. Try making it part of your management ritual.

As a corporate manager, I would often take this practice to the extreme. A regular feature in my staff meetings was "screwup of the week." If any member of my management team, including myself, had an embarrassing blunder, this was the time to go public, have a good laugh, and move on. This simple gesture sent a message to the team: Mistakes are an essential part of progress.

Each of the above is a simple starting point. But if done consistently over time, these practices can allow a leader to become a powerful force for liberating the intelligence from within an organization.

A LIBERATING FORCE

On January 1, 1831, William Lloyd Garrison, an antislavery activist, began a paper called *The Liberator*, of which he published 1,820 issues over thirty-five years. In *The Liberator*, Garrison spoke out eloquently and passionately against slavery and for the rights of America's black inhabitants. He wrote in the first edition: "I do not wish to think, or

speak, or write, with moderation . . . I am in earnest—I will not equiv-
ocate—I will not excuse—I will not retreat a single inch—and I will
be heard."

Garrison's fervor captures the essence of Multipliers. They aren't
necessarily social activists like Garrison, but they do activate intelligence. They aren't Tyrants, but they can be a bit despotic in their libera-
tion. Multipliers liberate people from the intimidation of hierarchical
organizations and the domination of tyrannical leaders. They see intelligence around them, and they release it into the organization so it can
be freely utilized at its highest point of contribution. They create an
environment where ideas can be heard and where intelligence can be
given, grown, and stretched through challenge.

THE MULTIPLIER FORMULA

THE TYRANT VERSUS THE LIBERATOR

TYRANTS create a tense environment that suppresses people's thinking and capability. As a result, people hold back, bring up safe ideas that the leader agrees with, and work cautiously.

LIBERATORS create an intense environment that requires people's best thinking and work. As a result, people offer their best and boldest thinking and give their best effort.

The Three Practices of the Liberator

1. *Create Space*
   - Release others by restraining yourself
   - Shift the ratio of listening to talking
   - Operate consistently
   - Level the playing field

2. *Demand Best Work*
   - Defend the standard
   - Distinguish best work from outcomes

3. *Generate Rapid Learning Cycles*
   - Admit and share mistakes
   - Insist on learning from mistakes

Becoming a Liberator

1. Play your chips
2. Label your opinions
3. Make your mistakes known

Unexpected Findings

1. The path of least resistance is often the path of tyranny. Because many organizations are skewed, a leader can be above average in an organization and still operate as a Tyrant.

2. Liberators maintain a duality of giving people permission to think while also creating an obligation for them to do their best work.

3. Multipliers are intense. Leaders who can discern and create the difference between a *tense* and an *intense* climate can access significantly more brainpower from their organizations.

CHAPTER 4

THE CHALLENGER

The number one difference between a Nobel prize
winner and others is not IQ or work ethic, but that they
ask bigger questions.

PETER DRUCKER

In 2005, Shai Agassi sat in a large auditorium in Davos, Switzerland, at the World Economic Forum. He was there as one of 200 Young Global Leaders, an elite group of up-and-coming world leaders, all under forty years of age. At the time, he was a top executive and board member at SAP and was assumed to be next in line for CEO. As he sat in the forum, he was asked a simple question, "What could you do to make the world a better place?" The question and the challenge stuck with him. He left SAP in 2007 and founded Better Place in Palo Alto, California.[1]

Shai started with a simple question: How do you run a country without oil? But initially the answers were far from simple. He first posed the questions and tested the ideas with his colleagues at Young Global Leaders and with a white paper to the WEF. He looked at alternative forms of transportation and worked on the question for six months in small groups. After several iterations, he could see the opportunity. After a year, he knew pursuing this opportunity was the right thing to do. He began building the team that would make it happen.

AN IDEA FOR A BETTER PLACE To build his team, he simply explained the opportunity as he saw it. This was nothing short of a chance to make the world a better place, which inspired the name for the company: Better Place.[2] He then explained the possibility. Known for his sharp intellect and ability to see around corners, Shai began to assemble the pieces of the story. He explained the logic supporting electricity as the most viable energy source for cars and took others through this same logic. Barak Hershkovitz, CTO for Better Place, said, "After a five minute conversation about the opportunity, I decided to leave my job and join him."

A CHALLENGE Not only did Shai explain the opportunity he saw, but he began to lay out the challenge. To make electric cars a viable option, someone would need to build the infrastructure for recharging or switching batteries. Someone would need to be the AT&T and build the network across a vast geography. After months of analysis, the team realized that battery charging could not be the most viable solution; they would have to build an infrastructure for rapid battery switching at stations much like gas stations. Shai issued the challenge to the team and began asking the difficult questions: "How can we change a battery in five minutes? . . . and how can we make it user-friendly? . . . and location-independent? . . . and car-independent? . . . and cheap so it can be scalable?" He turned the problem over to the team and gave them two months. The team then broke the challenge down into pieces and constructed a solution. Within three months, they had a working prototype—not for a battery switch in five minutes, but rather a solution to switch a battery in 1.5 minutes. It was beyond his outrageous expectations.

A POSSIBILITY "Shai is an expert in making the impossible possible," says one senior member of his team. "He breaks down the challenge in a way that makes you believe it can happen."

Barak recounts a pivotal moment for Better Place: "I was preparing for a critical meeting with one of the car makers. I knew they were skeptical about the solution we had developed, so I had developed a Plan B, which was a compromise that might be easier for them to adopt. Right before the critical meeting I told Shai that I had created, reluctantly, a Plan B. Shai asked me, 'Do you believe in what you are doing?' He paused. 'Is it the right solution?' He sensed my hesitation, and asked, 'Is there a better solution?' I told him that there wasn't a better solution, but that Plan B represented a compromise that would not work as well. Shai told me, 'Believe in what you do and stick with the truth. I'll back you up.' I stood up at the meeting with the car maker and gave the speech for the original solution, not the Plan B compromise. It must have been in the way I said it and in my conviction. But all of a sudden, the impossible became possible. The whole room was now in support for the original solution."

Shai is a master at defining opportunities that dare people to stretch beyond what they know how to do. This is one reason why Shai was listed in *Time* magazine's 100 Most Influential People list, published in a May 2009 issue. His team describes what it is like to work with such a Challenger:

> "He'll outstretch all your capabilities to make it happen. He is highly demanding, but you feel great.
>
> "You know you are signing up for something that will challenge you on a daily basis for many years to come. You will challenge yourself and all your capabilities.
>
> "Exhilarating, exhausting, challenging, gratifying."[3]
>
> "He's a big source of energy. He is a source of power and a tailwind for what we do."

Shai gets more out of people than they knew they had to give—and they love it. It appears the man who seeks to charge the world's electric cars has found a way to charge the people in his own organization.

Consider another company founder.

The Expert

Richard Palmer founded SMT Systems in the mid-1990s in the United Kingdom to build systems and tools for business process reengineering. Started as Richard's brainchild, the company's intellectual foundation was built from his expertise as a business process analyst and in expert systems. The process reengineering work appealed to Richard's sense of methodology and superior strategy, both developed through years of playing chess as a youth.

Not only was Richard one of England's youngest chess champions (holding a Master rating), but it was common knowledge throughout the company that he was a chess champion. It was typically the first thing people said about Richard. Chess champion and Oxford University graduate. He was clearly a genius and the chief genius in the company. While he gave the title of CEO to someone else, everyone knew Richard, who remained the chairman of the board, was still the one who called the shots on budget, pricing, products, compensation, and company strategy.

AN ARMY OF PAWNS The energy changes in a room when Richard enters. It is as if the headmaster has entered the school assembly. People begin to shrink. People react the way they might when the calculus teacher gives a surprise oral quiz, getting smaller—hoping he or she won't call on them and find them lacking. Despite the fact that everyone fears the attention will turn to them, the attention often just stays with Richard, who works to make sure he is seen as the expert and smartest person in the room.

In one executive management meeting, Richard put the company general counsel in the hot seat with a pop quiz about a technical distinction on a very specific legal code regarding corporate governance. Richard had become concerned that his general counsel didn't fully understand the nuances of this particular code that had to be reported to "the city," so he began launching questions. One by one, the general counsel answered them until the questions became more precise and delved into nuances and obscure scenarios. The general counsel looked puzzled, but answered the questions to the best of his knowledge. But, this didn't satisfy Richard. Richard left work just in time to stop by a WHSmith bookshop before it closed. He didn't buy just any governance book, he bought the 600-page manual on the most recently announced corporate governance codes. And, he didn't just look up the answer to the question he asked, he stayed up through the night reading the entire book. The following day, he called a meeting of the executive team. The topic for this emergency management meeting was, of course, this particular code. Richard professed his newfound knowledge and quite publicly let everyone know everything the general counsel got wrong.

BAD BISHOP Richard is a master of "The Gotcha" question. Richard only asks questions that he knows the answer to. He asks questions to test other people's knowledge and to make sure other people understand his point of view. One of his vice presidents said, "I can't think of a single time that he has asked a question when he didn't know the answer."

He is also a master of "The Stall" question, which he uses when he doesn't have the answer himself. He is known for asking frivolous questions during teleconferences to stall the conversation while he googles the answers to get ahead in the conversation. One such "stall" was during a meeting with an account team that was planning their sales proposal for a deal with British Telecom. The sales team was reviewing the proposed contract. Richard, who appeared to not yet know exactly how the contract should be worded, jumped in with, "How many of you have read British Telecom's field operations manual?" The document was 500 pages long and not your typical reading for a sales representative. Wondering if this was a trick question, the team tentatively confessed that they hadn't read it. Richard replied with, "How can you even understand this contract and sell to a BT if you haven't read the field operations manual?" The sales process came to a complete standstill while the entire account team, and Richard the founder and chairman of the board, read the manual. One team member said, "He wasn't the kind of leader who would say, 'I have an idea. Why don't we look in the manual to better understand the business and the terms of the contract?' Instead, he made us look ridiculous for not doing it."

FOOL'S MATE It is no surprise that really smart, talented people don't stay long in this organization. Some are asked to leave when the founder finds out they aren't as smart as he'd like. Others "quit and stay," giving up on the idea of making a meaningful contribution. The sharpest people leave because they see the wasted time and talent and know the organization can't grow beyond its founder. Although the company has been able to grow sales under Richard's leadership, most believe that the organization is inherently limited. They remark, "We'll never become a serious company."

One of these two founders operated as a Challenger. The other founder operated as a Know-It-All. This chapter is about the difference.

THE KNOW-IT-ALL VERSUS THE CHALLENGER

The approach of these two founders captures the essential difference between how Know-It-Alls and Challengers provide direction and pursue opportunities for their organization.

Diminishers operate as Know-It-Alls, assuming that their job is to know the most and to tell their organization what to do. The organization often revolves around what they know, with people wasting cycles trying to deduce what the boss thinks and how to—at least—look like they are executing accordingly. In the end, Diminishers place an artificial limit on what their organizations can accomplish. Because they are overly focused on what they know, they limit what their organization can achieve to what they themselves know how to do.

In setting direction for their organizations, Multipliers have a fundamentally different approach. Instead of knowing the answer, they play the role of the Challenger. They use their smarts to find the right opportunities for their organizations and challenge and stretch their organizations to get there. They aren't limited by what they themselves know. They push their teams beyond their own knowledge and that of the organization. As a result, they create organizations that deeply understand a challenge and have the focus and energy to confront it.

The Mind of a Multiplier

What are the assumptions that lie at the heart of these different approaches? Consider our two founders. What caused Shai to challenge his organization in a way that allowed others to do their very best thinking and best work? And why did other people's intelligence and capability stagnate around Richard? We know that both founders are highly intelligent, with a clear vision for their organizations and a passion for their work. But if we examine their approach to setting direction, we can distinguish two different logics at work.

Deeply embedded in Richard's logic is the assumption: *I need to have all the answers.* He sees this as the essence of his job as the leader. And if he doesn't know the answers, he needs to either find them himself or appear to know the answers. What does he do when he doesn't have the answer? He stalls until he can find it. He buys a book on corporate governance. He reads the operations manual. He googles the answer. He assumes his role is to know and to be the expert. It is an assumption that may have become entrenched in the years he studied expert systems.

If a leader holds the assumption that it is a leader's role to provide the answers and if the employees resign themselves to this mode of business, a downward Know-It-All spiral naturally follows. First, the leader provides all the answers. Second, subordinates wait for the directives they've come to expect. Third, the subordinates act on the leader's answers. Finally, the leader concludes *they would never have figured this out without me.* He or she sees evidence to support this belief and concludes: *it is obvious I need to tell others what to do.*

Shai's leadership at Better Place follows a different logic. He uses his intellect and energy on two things: first, asking the big questions and second, showing that a solution is possible. He understands the challenge at a deep enough level to believe a solution is possible. His assumption seems to be that *people get smarter by being challenged.* As people embrace the challenge, both their insights and the belief grows. Soon, the belief becomes infectious and the unsolvable problems become solvable. Antiquated arguments give way to new thinking and what once appeared to be roadblocks become interesting puzzles, which teams solve one by one.

If leaders have to spread their intelligence across asking the questions *and* finding all the answers, they will tend to ask questions they already know the answers to. Once a leader accepts that he or she doesn't have to have all the answers, he or she is free to ask much bigger, more provocative and, frankly, more interesting questions. They can pursue things they don't know how to do.

Let's look at another Challenger in action.

THE CHALLENGER

By 1995, the Oracle Corporation was headquartered in the affluent waterfront neighborhood of Redwood Shores on the San Francisco Peninsula in California. Oracle had begun retooling its products for the Internet, but the business strategy was still unclear. The challenge of figuring it out would fall to Ray Lane, Oracle's president, who had joined Oracle two years earlier and had grown the U.S. business from $571 million to $1.2 billion.

RAY'S REVOLUTION Ray decided to gather the top 250 leaders of the company from across the globe in a series of forums to educate them on the corporate strategy and to align the leadership team behind this strategy. Ray and the other senior executives, including CEO Larry Ellison and CFO Jeff Henley, prepared their strategy presentations and gathered the first group of thirty executives. They gave their presentations and held discussions, but as the week went on, the group became more and more confused. One VP spoke for the group when he said, "We aren't clear on the strategy. We just saw a lot of PowerPoint slides."

Ray and his team went back to the drawing board and did a major overhaul of their presentations. They invited another group of thirty executives. This time the feedback was different: it was an all out revolt. One of the executives took a risk and said, "Stop getting people together until there is a clear strategy!" The team was not buying what Ray and the rest of the team were selling.

INDEPENDENCE DAY The senior executive team quickly regrouped at Ray's house on their first available day, the Fourth of July. They realized the global business had become more complex and diverse than they originally thought and that they couldn't build this strategy alone at corporate. They decided to take a fundamentally different approach. Ray and the executive team started out trying to tell others all the answers. They switched to sharing the fundamental questions, trends, and assumptions that were shaping their views.

When they came back together with the next forum of leaders, Ray and the other executives shared what they saw happening in the business and where they saw the world going. Ray seeded the opportunities that these trends would present for Oracle and presented a framework for a strategy—four key transformations needed in the business. And then with this broad stroke of his brush, he stopped telling and started asking, "Are these the transformations needed in the business?" and "Which of our assumptions about the future might be wrong?"

Ray gave the group a challenge to fill in the blanks. The team would have two days to examine each of the four transformations, identify milestones, and pinpoint the implications for the business, and then pass their thinking on to the next group of leaders who would go further. The group did exactly that, advancing the thinking of the executive team and then handing off their work to the next group of executives. The group reveled in their collective success and left the forum knowing that they had begun something big. The process continued until all SVPs and VPs had been involved. Each group challenged the work that had been done before them. They took their task seriously, turning the strategy upside down and sideways as they looked for holes, logic flaws, and vulnerabilities. In the end, they emerged with both a validation and a refinement of the collective thinking. The momentum was building.

THE CONVENTION Ray and the other executives culminated this process by convening the entire leadership team of the company. The executive team unveiled the strategic intent of the organization and the transformations needed in the business. The reaction of the global leadership team was overwhelming enthusiasm and optimism, knowing they would be making business history. The strategy was fresh and compelling, yet it was familiar to them because they had co-created it and could see their fingerprints on it.

When the meeting was divided into regional breakouts, the scene was far from typical. Instead of a discussion about "why this won't work in Europe, the Middle East, and Africa (EMEA)," the conversation in the EMEA breakout room was almost boisterous with questions like, "What is the first step?" and "Where can we start implementing this in Germany?" The scene in the Japanese breakout room said it all. They discussed the strategy and its implications for Japan. And then, with quiet fervor, they began to organize as if they were going to battle.

What was unveiled in the meeting and the breakout sessions was a manifestation and statement of the collective will of the organization. Under Ray Lane and Larry Ellison's leadership, the organization forged ahead to execute this strategic intent, propelling Oracle into the lead position in the late 1990s for enterprise computing in the Internet world. From 1996 to 2000, Oracle grew from $4.2 billion to $10.1 billion, more than doubling revenues.

Ray Lane began with an honest attempt to sell a strategy to the organization. But he emerged a more powerful leader as he first seeded the opportunity, and then laid down the stretch challenge for the organization. He didn't set the direction; he ensured the direction was set. He operated as a Challenger.

THE THREE PRACTICES OF THE CHALLENGER

How does the Challenger engage the full brainpower of the organization? Among the Multipliers we studied in our research, we found three common practices. Multipliers: 1) seed the opportunity; 2) lay down a challenge; and 3) generate belief. We'll examine each in turn.

I. Seed the Opportunity

Multipliers understand that people grow through challenge. They understand that intelligence grows by being stretched and tested. So even if the leader has a clear vision of the direction, he or she doesn't just give it to people. Multipliers don't just give answers. They provide just enough information to provoke thinking and to help people discover and see the opportunity for themselves. They begin a process of discovery.

We'll outline a few of the ways that Multipliers seed opportunity and begin the discovery process.

Show the Need

One of the best ways to seed an opportunity is to allow someone else to discover it for him- or herself. When people can see the need for themselves, they develop a deep understanding of the issues, and quite often, all the leader needs to do is get out of their way and let them solve the problem.

The Bennion Center, on the University of Utah campus, was established to encourage students to engage in community service projects and activism while in college. Irene Fisher, the center's director for fourteen years, was hopeful that the students would sign up for some of the city's toughest problems.

Instead of making a speech or just selling her vision of service to the poorest members of the community, Irene invited students to take a leadership position and organize other students to work with the community. She took them downtown into the inner-city community so they could see the needs for themselves. They walked the streets and observed the plight of the homeless. They visited shelters and talked with single mothers struggling to get by. Because they saw the needs for themselves, they became passionate and curious about how to create change, and learned rapidly in the process. As their involvement level grew, these student leaders assumed more and more challenging roles. She noted, "University students are pretty smart. Once they see something they start asking questions. Our students asked a lot of questions and then went to work." Irene seeded the opportunity and allowed the students to take the challenge. Irene added, "I don't see myself as a challenger per se. I think of creating the opportunity for people to see the challenge so they can respond to it."

The Bennion Center is still thriving today, built on the assumption that you don't get the most out of people if you just tell them what to do. You get full effort if you help people discover opportunity and, then, challenge themselves.

Challenge the Assumptions

Multipliers ask the questions that challenge the fundamental assumptions in an organization and disrupt the prevailing logic. Renowned management guru and strategy professor C.K. Prahalad is known for asking the questions that challenge the fundamental assumptions of an organization. He understands that strategy is about understanding and questioning assumptions. When working with management teams in leading corporations, C.K. has a penchant for asking the unsettling questions that rattle their assumptions and enable them to see market opportunities and threats in a different light.

In working with the Phillips Corporation, a multinational manufacturing company, and after carefully interviewing each member of the executive team to uncover their core assumptions about the business and the tensions in the organization, he could see that they had an assumed invincibility in the market. C.K. formulated a plan. When he arrived at their executive strategy offsite, he began with a fictitious article he'd written that might appear in *The New York Times* speculating a bankruptcy at Phillips. He then launched the following questions: What changes in the current competitive landscape would devastate Phillips's revenue stream? What if companies A and B merged? What market changes could lead to a bankruptcy? What is your game plan if it happens? The room became tensely silent. He had shaken their beliefs upon which the current business strategy was based. With the full interest of the executive team, he guided the discussion as they began to explore the answers.

Reframe Problems

Multipliers understand the power of an opportunity. As Peter Block, consulting guru and author, observed, "the most powerful work is done in response to an opportunity not in response to a problem."

Multipliers analyze problems, but they also reframe them to show the opportunity presented by the challenges.

Consider how Alan G. Lafley, when he was CEO of Procter & Gamble, reframed the problems of generating revenue growth from new product R&D as part of his overall revitalization of the company.

As Larry Huston and Nabil Sakkab explain in their *Harvard Business Review* article "Connect and Develop," the "invent-it-themselves" model was no longer allowing P&G to sustain a high level of top-line growth. At $25 billion the company could still manage to do it, but beyond $50 billion it was impossible and P&G lost half of their market cap as their stock fell from $118 to $52 a share.

Rather than falling into the trap of doing more of the same, Lafley developed a new strategy of sourcing their innovation from the outside. The shift was from "not invented here" to "proudly invented elsewhere." Rather than thinking of innovation as "invention" where the R&D has to be done in your own physical labs, Lafley looked for ways to join forces with people in their supply chain whom they could partner with to innovate more rapidly.

For example, Huston and Sakkab relate, when the idea emerged to produce Pringles potato chips with pictures and words printed on the crisps themselves, P&G had to decide whether to create an end-to-end solution from scratch, or whether to find an innovative solution somewhere within their partner network. In the past, bringing a new product to market represented a two-year investment. But with Lafley's new reframe, they could see a smarter path.

In the case of the Pringles, they "created a technology brief that defined the problems [they] needed to solve, and [they] circulated it throughout [their] global networks of individuals and institutions to discover if anyone in the world had a ready-made solution. It was through [their] European network that [they] discovered a small bakery in Bologna, Italy, run by a university professor who also manufactured baking equipment."[4] The professor's innovation allowed P&G to get to market in half the time and at a fraction of the cost of inventing the solutions in-house. The product was an immediate hit. It led the Pringles division to enjoy double-digit growth for the next two years.

Create a Starting Point

Multipliers provide a starting point, but not a complete solution. By offering a starting point, they generate more questions than answers. These questions then encourage their team to fully define the opportunity while giving them confidence that they are building on a solid foundation.

Ray Lane and Oracle's top executives created the skeleton of a strategic framework and then asked groups of senior leaders to systematically and collaboratively work to complete the whole strategy.

When a Challenger has successfully seeded an opportunity, other people can see the opportunity for themselves. And because the opportunity has been planted but is not fully grown, others are taken through a process of discovery. This process of exploration and discovery sparks intellectual curiosity and begins to generate energy for the challenge. And because the answers are clearly not formed, people know "there is still something for me to do" and they can step in to be involved.

II. Lay Down a Challenge

Once an opportunity is seeded and intellectual energy is created, Multipliers establish the challenge at hand in such a way that it creates a huge stretch for an organization. While Diminishers create a huge gap between what they know and what other people know, Multipliers create a vacuum that draws people into the challenge. They establish a compelling challenge that creates tension. People see the tension and the size of the stretch and are intrigued and, perhaps, even puzzled.

Mission Impossible

Matt McCauley took the reins of Gymboree, a $790 million children's retailer headquartered in San Francisco, at the age of thirty-three, after coming through the ranks of planning and inventory management. This made Matt not only the youngest CEO to head Gymboree in its thirty-year history but also the youngest CEO of a company in Wall Street's Russell 2000 index.

McCauley used his youth to keep him open to the ideas of others. "I love to riff and bounce ideas off of people. Regardless of what their function is, [Gymboree employees] are all talented, bright people," says McCauley.[5] Matt had been a pole vaulter in college. He set one bar at seventeen feet, six inches, which is what he could clear, but he always kept a second bar set at twenty feet—the world record at the time—to remind himself of what was possible. Matt took this same approach at work.

RAISING THE BAR When Matt took over as president he had the benefit of a recently rejuvenated product line but the challenge of some sloppy business operations. He saw an opportunity not only to grow sales, but to vastly increase net income per share, which was then at $0.69 per share. Using his deep knowledge of operations and inventory optimization, he estimated the upside opportunity, and then went to the board and told them he believed the company could achieve $1.00 per share. The board members laughed, but Matt remained convinced of the opportunity.

As Matt met with his management team, he explained his rationale for the growth opportunity in both sales and earnings per share. He took them through the calculations for sales and expense optimizations that he had been studying for the last five years and asked if they could indeed be achieved. He then threw out "Mission Impossible"—a net income of $1.00. He asked each member of his management team this question: "What would be your Mission Impossible?" As the management team caught the enthusiasm of this high-bar approach, they began to ask the entire organization to do the same. Soon every person inside this 9,500-person organization had a Mission Impossible goal—a crazy aspiration. It appeared that being asked to identify their personal Mission Impossible ignited the charge to make it possible.

CLEARING THE BAR A year later Matt announced to the board, to Wall Street, and to every employee in Gymboree that they had achieved not just the "Mission Impossible" goal of $1.00 per share, but $1.19 per share, which represented a 72 percent improvement over the previous fiscal year.

Fueled by this accomplishment, what did Matt do next? He set the bar higher and suggested to the board that they could achieve $2.00 per share. This time the board thought it was outrageous. But he turned to his organization for support, sharing his Mission Impossible task and once again asking every person to create their personal Mission Impossible needed to achieve $2.00 per share. In fiscal year 2007, they delivered $2.15 per share, an 80 percent improvement.

Again Matt went to the board to suggest $3 per share. One year later he announced $2.67 per share and two years later, in 2008, an incredible $3.21 per share. That is a more than 50 percent increase in earnings per share year over year and an almost fivefold increase in four years.

This young Challenger CEO used his deep knowledge of the business to see both an opportunity and a path for achieving unheard-of levels of business performance. He articulated this opportunity and laid down the challenge for the organization. He then asked each person to join him in attempting the impossible and to analyze how they might achieve it. By setting the bar high, he gave people permission to rethink the business. By asking them to create their personal Mission Impossible, he allowed them to embrace and step into the challenge themselves. And by acknowledging the impossible nature of the mission, he gave people permission to try without fear of failure.

How does a Multiplier achieve this level of stretch without breaking an organization? How do you create intrigue rather than apprehension? In our research, we found that Multipliers achieve this energizing stretch in three ways.

First, they extend a clear and concrete challenge. Then they ask the hard questions that need to be answered to achieve the challenge, but, most important, *they* don't answer them. They let others fill in the blanks.

Extend a Concrete Challenge

Sean Mendy works as a director of an after-school program in East Palo Alto, California, a city that in 1992 had the highest per-capita murder rate in the United States and a city where dropping out of high school is a norm. Sean himself faced many challenges growing up, but went on to attend and graduate from Cornell University.

After graduation, Sean decided to spend a year at the Boys and Girls Club of the Peninsula. Four years later, he can't bring himself to leave. Even now, after being accepted into a graduate program at Stanford, you can find him doing his homework at the club beside youth half his age. With a journey like Sean's, he has ample reason to tell the teens he works with what they need to do to succeed. But, instead of telling, he challenges.

When Sean first met Tajianna Robinson (or Taji), she was a shy and hesitant twelve-year-old. When she reluctantly shook his outstretched hand, he stopped her and with a big smile said, "You know there are three things you might want to do when you meet someone. First, look them in the eye. Second, give them a firm hand. Third, shake their hand up and down three full times." Taji was appalled but intrigued.

Sean continued to extend small, specific challenges to her. He asked Taji if she would take a newspaper class. She did. Then he encouraged her to write a main article for the school paper, meet regularly with a writing tutor, and learn how to write a great essay. Again, she did. Next, he encouraged her to raise the bar and compete in her school's Scholar of the Year competition. She won!

Sean extends these challenges by asking the youth hard questions and then giving them the space to think and respond. As Taji put it, "He taught me to think for myself." This allows youth like Taji to strengthen intellectual muscles and build the confidence they need to tackle the hardest challenges.

Early on with Taji, Sean looked her in the eye and asked, "If you could get out of this environment, what would you do?" There was a long silence. Finally Taji said, "I'd go to college." Sean responded, "What would it take for you to do that?" After several moments of reflection, her eyes lit up, "I'd need to get into the right high school!" They set a goal for Taji to earn a scholarship to one of the top-tier prep schools in the surrounding area. Sean asked, "Where should we start?"

Taji led the process, but together they figured out which schools would be the best fit. They completed applications and prepared for her high school interviews. Then, the night before one of the biggest interviews, Taji's family left her at home to do her homework while they went out for a drive. As the family pulled up to a stop sign, a gunman approached the car, firing multiple bullets into the vehicle that was transporting three small children. Taji's older cousin was shot in the back, and her six-year-old sister was shot in the leg. Nobody died, but it was traumatic in every conceivable way.

The next morning Sean suggested Taji might want to reschedule the high school interview they had planned. But through her emotions she yelled, "This is how I am going to get out of here! This is what I need to do to have the kind of life I want. And this is how I can help my family and make sure it doesn't happen again!" She wiped her tears, went to the interview, and blew away everyone she met. Tajianna was accepted to four competitive preparatory schools, earning full scholarships to each. She now attends Sacred Heart, a private school in Atherton, California, and has flourished into a resilient, motivated, and strikingly bright fourteen-year-old girl.

Out of the seventeen students in Sean's eighth-grade program, twelve have received scholarships to prestigious prep schools and the other five have entered rigorous college-track programs. Sean served as a Challenger, helping these youth raise their aspiration level and build the mental agility they would need to get and stay on a course of success.

Whether it is Matt McCauley at Gymboree extending the $2 challenge, or Shai Agassi inviting his team to find a way to change a battery in less than five minutes, or Sean Mendy issuing the college-bound challenge, our research showed that Multipliers use their intelligence to make challenges concrete for others. These challenges become tangible and measurable, allowing people to assess their performance. And by making a challenge real, they allow others to visualize the achievement and communicate the confidence that the organization has the collective brainpower required. This confidence is essential because the challenge will demand the entire organization to extend beyond its current reach and capability.

Ask the Hard Questions

Diminishers give answers. Good leaders ask questions. Multipliers ask the really hard questions. They ask the questions that challenge people not only to think but to rethink. They ask questions so immense that people can't answer them based on their current knowledge or where they currently stand. To answer these questions, the organization must learn.

Enabled by these big questions, a vacuum is created. It is a vacuum between what people know and what they need to know to answer the question. It also is a vacuum between what they can currently do and what they need to be able to do. This vacuum creates a deep tension in the organization and raises a need to reduce that tension. It is like a rubber band that is stretched to its limit. One side needs to move toward the other to reduce the tension.

Matt McCauley at Gymboree created this forward pull when he asked each member of his organization, "What is your Mission Impossible?" Shai Agassi created this tension at Better Place when he asked,

"How would we build an infrastructure to switch batteries from any electric car anywhere in the world, and do it cheaply?"

Let Others Fill in the Blanks

How do Multipliers get people to step into a challenge? They shift the burden of the thinking to others. Initially, when they establish a concrete challenge, the burden of the thinking sits with them as the leader. But by asking the hard questions and inviting others to fill in the blanks, they are shifting the burden of thinking onto their people. The intellectual onus now sits with their team to understand the challenge and find a solution. It is in this shift that the Multiplier creates intelligence and energy around him or herself.

After assuming leadership of a new division in a large consumer electronics company in Korea, the CEO called his management team together and informed them of his goals to be number one in the market and to become a magnet company attracting top college graduates. He was clear that the trajectory for the organization would not be incremental. He had a vision of something big. He then engaged a broad array of stakeholders in analyzing how to achieve the number one position. The coalition included key executives, founding family members, and outside consultants. Assembling the coalition, he seeded the opportunity and posed the difficult questions such as, "Why are we in this business?" and "Do we deserve to be in this business?" and "What would it take to be better than our competition?"

These questions cut to the bones of the organization and stirred up chaos. Yet he never backed down. The tension forced the team to generate answers. He asked the hard questions and then let the team fill in the blanks. As they did, he maintained a tight time frame. He said, "I don't need 100 percent answers. I need a 30 percent answer in two days. Give me a 30 percent answer so we can talk about it and decide if it makes sense for you to find a 50 percent answer. And if we get there, we'll block two months to get a 100 percent answer."

In the end there were clear answers. The process took months and was scrappy, but it built the intellectual muscle and energy the organization needed for the challenge.

Laying down a challenge means more than directing people to do it. It includes asking the hard questions that no one yet has the answers to and then backing off so that the people within the organization have the space to think through the questions, take ownership, and find the answers.

When a Multiplier has successfully laid down the challenge, people see the stretch, are intrigued, and become intellectually engaged. The burden of thinking has been shifted to the organization. This process of ownership and stretch continues to build energy by creating the intellectual muscle for the challenge.

III. Generate Belief

By seeding the opportunity and laying down a challenge, people are interested in what is possible. But this isn't enough to create movement. Multipliers generate belief—the belief that the impossible is actually possible. It isn't enough that people see and understand the stretch; they need to actually stretch themselves.

The following are a few ways we discovered that Multipliers produce this belief in their organizations.

Helicopter Down

One way Multipliers generate belief is by taking the challenge down to the ground level. K.R. Sridhar, CEO of Bloom Energy, whose vision is to produce power generators for homes and businesses at half the carbon emissions of traditional power generators, explained, "The direction needs to be improbable but not impossible. It can't just exist at 30,000 feet. It has to be at the 1,000 foot level. It is irresponsible to ask your team to do something if the CEO exposure is only at the 30,000 foot level. You have to take it down and show that it can be done. You have to show them a pathway and show why it can be done. You only need to do this once to create the belief." By "helicoptering" down to reality, Multipliers create a meaningful proof point that a bold challenge can be successfully met.

Lay Out a Path

Shai Agassi is a master at making the impossible seem possible. When he was leading the technology organization at SAP, he challenged the team to build a rapid deployment package that would allow a mid-size company to install SAP in less than seven days. This was unheard of, as a typical SAP implementation is measured in months, not days. But he didn't just issue this outrageous challenge, he helped find a path. He and the team analyzed historical implementations and found that 90 percent of the implementations shared the same features, and discovered that this configuration works for most mid-size companies. With this insight, the team could see a path toward a seven-day implementation program, and they proceeded to make it happen.

Co-Create the Plan

When people create the plan that they eventually will implement, belief in its viability will be inherently high. Led by Ray Lane in 1996, Oracle not only built a strategic intent, it also built a deep belief within the organization that Oracle could lead the Internet era. Because 250 senior leaders were given the opportunity to co-create the corporate strategy, they understood the challenge ahead and knew what actions would be necessary to achieve it. They had built the collective will and energy needed to execute. The organization was ready to take the challenge.

Orchestrate an Early Win

Sometimes, the temptation exists for leaders to tackle too many problems all at once. Our research showed that Multipliers begin with small, early wins and use those to generate belief toward the greater stretch challenges.

Consider Nobel Prize winner Wangari Maathai. In her words, "I was hearing many Nairobi women complain that they didn't have enough firewood, they were also complaining that they did not have enough water. 'Why not plant trees?' I asked them. And so they just started, *very, very, very small.* And before too long they started showing each other. Communities began empowering each other to plant trees for their own needs."[6]

From just seven original trees planted by Wangari on June 5, 1977, on World Environment Day, the Green Belt movement has successfully planted more than 40 million trees in Africa. And of course, the movement goes beyond trees. Wangari has written, "Many people don't understand that the tree is just an entry point. It is an easy point. Because it is something that people understand. It is something people can do. It is not very expensive to do it. And you don't need too much technology to do it. But once we get into the community through tree planting, we deal with a lot of other issues. We deal with issues of governance, issues of human rights, issues of conflicts and peace, [and] issues of long-term resource management."

Senior leaders in corporations can generate belief about significant challenges by orchestrating small, early wins.

When the Multiplier has generated belief in what is possible, the weight shifts and the organization is willing to leave the realm of the known and venture into the unknown.

The Academy Award–winning documentary *Man on Wire* chronicles the feat of renowned high-wire artist Philippe Petit in 1974 as he walked a tightrope stretched 140 feet across the expanse between the 1,368-foot-high Twin Towers of the World Trade Center in New York City. In the movie, Petit explains the moment of truth when he stood on the edge of one tower with his back foot on the building and his front foot on the cable. He recalled, "I had to make a decision of shifting my weight from one foot anchored to the building to the foot anchored on the wire. This is probably the end of my life to step on that wire! On the other hand, something I could not resist . . . called me up on that cable."

I have seen this shift of weight happen many times inside organizations. You can almost feel the energy of the organization begin to tip in a new direction. This shift happens when an individual or organization has fully embraced a challenge and has generated the belief in what is possible. It is not the Multiplier who whips up this belief. Rather, it is the challenge he or she has issued that generates this commitment. This challenge process builds the intellectual muscle, the emotional energy, and the collective intent to move forward. Multipliers orchestrate the process needed to shift the weight of an organization.

THE DIMINISHER'S APPROACH TO SETTING DIRECTION

In contrast to Multipliers, Diminishers have a fundamentally different approach to providing direction. Instead of using their intelligence to enable people to stretch toward a future opportunity, they give directions in a way that showcases their superior knowledge. Instead of seeding an opportunity and laying out a believable challenge, Diminishers tell and test. Like the stereotypical Know-It-All, they tell people what they know, tell people how to do their jobs, and test other people's knowledge to see if they are doing it right.

TELL WHAT THEY KNOW. Diminishers consider themselves thought leaders and readily share their knowledge; however, they rarely share it in a way that invites contribution. They tend to sell their ideas rather than learning what others know. One manager in Europe "took up all the oxygen in the room" by talking endlessly about *his ideas*. A peer said of him, "He is so busy sharing what he thinks, there is no space for anyone else." A direct report added this insight, "I have worked in the same department with him for ten years, and he has never asked me a question. Not once. Not ever. I have occasionally heard him ask a question to the universe, 'I wonder why we do X?' but even then he fills the silence with his own thoughts about the answer."

TEST WHAT YOU KNOW. When Diminishers do actually engage others, to no surprise, it is as an auditor. They want to verify that you understand what they know. They ask questions to make a point rather than to access greater insight or to generate collective learning. Like Richard Palmer, the founder discussed earlier, they are masters of the "gotcha" question. Diminishers leave people stressed, but unstretched.

TELL PEOPLE HOW TO DO THEIR JOBS. Rather than shifting responsibility to other people, Diminishers stay in charge and tell others—in detail— how to do their jobs. They assume the senior thinker posture, giving themselves permission to generate both the questions and the answers. One such Diminisher was Chip Maxwell, an executive producer on a major motion picture production set. Despite the fact that the director had carefully assembled a world-class team of talent, Chip was constantly interfering in the team's work, routinely bypassing the director to tell his staff exactly how to do their jobs. The director of photography abruptly resigned in the middle of filming, claiming that if Chip seemed to know how to light the shot better than he did, then maybe he could be the DP. This award-winning DP knew the number of lights needed, and he certainly knew where to put them. He also knew his talents could be better used on another film.

Diminishers often unintentionally shut down the intelligence of others. Most Diminishers have built their careers on their own expertise and have been rewarded for their superior knowledge. For many, it is not until they reach a career plateau or crisis—or the director of photography quits in the middle of filming—that they begin to recognize that their base assumptions are inaccurate and are limiting themselves and others.

A colleague of mine recently took an IQ test and received a score of 144. He was exuberant and claimed that he was just one point shy of certified genius status. No doubt he was envisioning his welcome letter from Mensa. On learning of our research, his enthusiasm became a bit dampened: "Wow. I have worked all my life to prove I am a genius, and just at the point that I can say that I am, I learn that it doesn't even matter anymore!"

Of course, this is only half right. Raw mental horsepower is still relevant. But the most powerful leaders are those who not only have this mental horsepower themselves, but also know how to multiply it by accessing and stretching other people's intelligence. Consider the difference between a leader who yearns for an additional IQ point to take their IQ to 145, official Genius Level, and leaders who use their intelligence to add an IQ point to every person in their organization! What could your organization accomplish if every person became effectively "one point smarter?"

There are times when a leader is so knowledgeable and personally brilliant that it seems tempting for them to provide directives centered in what they know. However, in the end, Know-It-Alls limit what their organization can achieve to what they themselves know how to do. Under their leadership, the organization never leverages its full intelligence, and the true capacity of the organization is idled away or becomes consumed by the "fire drill" of figuring out what the boss thinks.

HOW THE CHALLENGER
ACHIEVES RESOURCE LEVERAGE

Why do Challengers get more from their resources? By playing the Challenger instead of the Know-It-All, they access more brains, get those brains working faster, and earn the full discretionary effort of their people. Once they have a clear view of latent opportunities and challenges, they understand that there are no resources worthy of waste. Wisdom tells them that it is imperative to engage all intelligence and capability in service to these opportunities.

The following chart demonstrates why a Know-It-All leaves so much intelligence on the table while Challengers pull so much from their people.

Know-It-Alls		Challengers	
What They Do	*What They Get*	*What They Do*	*What They Get*
Give directives that showcase "their" knowledge	Distracted efforts as people vie for the attention of the boss Idle cycles in the organization as people wait to be told what to do or to see if the boss will change direction again An organization that doesn't want to get ahead of the boss	Define opportunities that challenge people to go beyond what they know how to do	Collective intent toward the same overarching opportunity Rapid cycles and accelerated problem solving without the initiation of the formal leader People's discretionary effort and intellectual energy to take on the toughest organizational challenges

When leaders operate as Challengers, teams are able to accelerate their performance. Because the organization does not have to wait for the leader to think of it first, they can solve tougher problems at an accelerated rate. Because people understand the context, they can act for themselves rather than wait to be told or approved. Consider the contrast in impact that this Diminisher and this Multiplier had on the productivity and velocity of their organizations.

A DIMINISHER CREATES IDLE CYCLES. A highly intelligent vice president at a major global technology firm was accustomed to a fast-paced and demanding environment. He was a competitor in the market who never stopped challenging himself and others. However, after transferring to a division led by a classic Know-It-All, he found himself idle most of the time. He said, "I spend most of my time waiting for my boss to make decisions. In the meantime, I can't do much else. I am essentially working part time. I'm bored, but I am enjoying taking sailing lessons!" This vice president was ready for high-speed battle but was relegated to easy sailing.

A MULTIPLIER CREATES RAPID CYCLES. Barak Hershkovitz, previously referenced, left a comfortable job to work as the CTO for Better Place, where his new CEO laid down the challenge for him before he even started work. Barak said, "I did more in one year at Better Place than I did in twenty years at my previous company. I'm not a Gantt chart pusher. I can work extremely fast because I don't get punished for mistakes. We work fast forward."

Because they are encouraged to be "smarter than the leader," people can stop competing for idea validation and instead commit themselves to the challenge. And the result is that intelligence grows—individually and collectively. The collective intent built within the organization enables the whole group to break through challenges no single leader, however intelligent, could have.

This understanding leads to a key question: how does someone provide direction like Shai Agassi at Better Place or Ray Lane at Oracle? How does someone go from a Know-It-All to a Challenger?

BECOMING A CHALLENGER

A Serious Case of Curiosity

Becoming a Challenger starts with developing an overactive imagination and a serious case of curiosity. In our research, we analyzed how Multipliers and Diminishers were rated against forty-eight leadership practices. It is not surprising that the highest-rated practice for Multipliers was "Intellectual Curiosity." Multipliers create genius in others because they are fundamentally curious and spark learning around them. This curiosity takes the form of an insatiable need for deep organizational understanding. The question "why" is at the core of their thinking. They ponder possibilities. They want to learn from people around them. At the heart of any challenge is intellectual curiosity: *I wonder if we could do the impossible?*

How does one become more curious? Thirty minutes watching (or in this case walking with) a young child will provide a good answer.

I recall a particular walk with my daughter, who was three years old at the time. It was one of those walks designed to relax both parent and child. But it managed to do the opposite. As we walked through the neighborhood, my daughter looked at everything and wanted to know "Why?" She asked, "Why is the dog barking?" and "Why is the road cracked?" and "Why do the cars go so fast?" This continued for some time. The questions got harder, and I was now running out of answers. I wondered how long this could go on. In an attempt to maintain my sanity and satisfy my own curiosity, I started counting the number of times my daughter asked "why?" during our little walk. At the current rate, I thought she might just break twenty-five. I stopped counting at eighty.

When deeply rooted in a mindset of curiosity, one is ready to begin working as a Challenger. Here are several starting points.

The Starting Block

1. GO EXTREME WITH QUESTIONS. Most executives are barraged with questions, constantly responding to others seeking their opinion. The nature of the executive role makes it easy to stay rooted in answer mode and to be the boss. The first step in this journey is to stop answering questions and begin asking them.

Several years ago I was commiserating with a colleague at work, Brian Spoutz, about how I had become horribly bossy with my children and was frustrated. I detailed a typical evening at my house where I barked orders at my young children: "Get ready for bed. Stop that. Put on your pajamas. Brush your teeth. Pick up your toys." Brian was also a parent of young children and gave me some advice. He listened carefully and said, "Liz, I have a challenge for you. Tonight when you go home, I want you to only speak to your children in the form of questions. No orders. No statements. Just questions." I was naturally intrigued. He said, "I think you might find that your children know exactly what they need to do." I agreed to take the challenge. He cautioned, "Only asking questions will feel awkward, but go all the way—nothing but questions for at least an hour or two."

That night when it was time for bed, I asked my children, "What time is it?" They responded with "bedtime." I then asked, "What do we do at bedtime?" They responded with, "We get on our pajamas and we brush our teeth." I continued the question routine with, "Well then, who is ready for bed?" They scampered to get on their pajamas and brush their teeth. I stood in the hallway in shock. The rest of the evening proceeded in a similar fashion, with me asking them leading questions and them responding with remarkable understanding and eagerness to act.

I reported this amazing experience to Brian the next day at work. He encouraged me to keep it up, not necessarily asking questions 100 percent of the time, but beginning to settle into a comfortable level. I did this and found that it transformed the way I operated as a parent. And it most certainly spilled over to how I managed at work. I have issued this same challenge to many leaders and have seen it transform their leadership as they shifted their balance and began asking more and telling less. It has helped them draw out the intelligence of people around them and guide others through a challenge.

Take the Extreme Question Challenge to shift from Know-It-All into Challenger mode. Start with 100 percent. Try it at home—you might find that your children (or housemates) are good guinea pigs and great teachers! At work, take the first step by finding a meeting that you can lead solely with questions. You might be surprised at what people around you already know.

2. TAKE A BUS TRIP. University of Michigan professor Noel Tichy tells a story about an executive at GE who found a creative way to seed a challenge and help his organization see a need in the marketplace.[7] When Tom Tiller took over the failing appliance division at GE, the division was losing money, slashing its workforce, and hadn't released a new product in years. Tom loaded forty people from his management team onto a rented bus and headed for the Atlanta Kitchen and Bath Show. The group was to find trends and needs, and generate new product ideas that would keep the plant alive. The group developed a new line of products and turned around the division, from a staggering loss to a $10 million profit.

There are many ways to take a bus trip. Irene Fisher of the Bennion Center took people into the inner city so they could see the needs of the poor firsthand. As a corporate manager, you might visit a customer's factory floor to watch how a customer actually uses your product. You can take your team down to the local mall to watch people shop. But go together on a bus trip. Help people see the need that must get met. Make it a learning experience that will reveal that need, create energy, and ignite a fire within your organization.

3. TAKE A MASSIVE BABY STEP. The corporate world has a plethora of names for this: Create an early win, deliver a symbolic victory, and—the favorite—pick the low-hanging fruit. But the problem is that most leaders do this in isolation. They pick a small group to run a pilot, which catches the attention of the management but don't have the visibility to get the attention of the entire organization. Instead, do it en masse. Make it visible. Create a conference room pilot for a new technology and hold an open house. Win back an important customer through the efforts of a cross-functional task force. Get the entire organization to take a small, first step. But do it together, en masse, so everyone can see the results and start to believe that something great is possible. This belief is what will shift the weight of the organization out onto that high wire.

A GOOD STRETCH

Jimmy Carter said, "If you have a task to perform and are vitally interested in it, excited and challenged by it, then you will exert maximum energy. But in the excitement, the pain of fatigue dissipates, and the exuberance of what you hope to achieve overcomes the weariness." Our research showed that Multipliers make challenges both provocative and plausible, attracting others to join them and offer their full capability, both intellectually and emotionally. Their approach generates the collective will and stretch needed to undertake the most paramount of challenges.

What is this like for the people who are willing to sign up? It is "Exhilarating, exhausting, challenging, gratifying." This means that Multipliers get contributions from their people that far surpass what they thought they had to give, and it is this concomitant exhilaration that makes people sign up again and again.

THE MULTIPLIER FORMULA

THE KNOW-IT-ALL VERSUS THE CHALLENGER

KNOW-IT-ALLS give directives that showcase how much they know. As a result they limit what their organization can achieve to what they themselves know how to do. The organization uses its energy to deduce what the boss thinks.

CHALLENGERS define opportunities that challenge people to go beyond what they know how to do. As a result they get an organization that understands the challenge and has the focus and energy to take it on.

The Three Practices of the Challenger

1. *Seed the Opportunity*
   - Show the need
   - Challenge the assumptions
   - Reframe problems
   - Create a starting point

2. *Lay Down a Challenge*
   - Extend a concrete challenge
   - Ask the hard questions
   - Let others fill in the blanks

3. *Generate Belief in What Is Possible*
   - Helicopter down
   - Lay out a path
   - Co-create the plan
   - Orchestrate an early win

Becoming a Challenger

1. Ask a leading question
2. Take a bus trip
3. Take a massive baby step

Unexpected Findings

1. Even when leaders have a clear view of the future, there are advantages to simply seeding the opportunities.

2. Challengers have full range of motion: they can see and articulate the big thinking and ask the big questions, but they can also connect that to the specific steps needed to create movement.

3. If you ask people to take on the impossible in the right way, it can actually create more safety than if you ask for something easier.

CHAPTER 5

THE DEBATE MAKER

It is better to debate a decision without settling it than settling a decision without debating it.

JOSEPH JOUBERT

How leaders make decisions is profoundly influenced by how they engage and leverage the resources around them. Our research has shown that Diminishers tend to make decisions solo or with a small inner circle. As a result, they not only underutilize the intelligence around them, but they also leave the organization spinning instead of executing. Multipliers make decisions by first engaging people in debate—not only to achieve sound decisions, but also to develop collective intelligence and to ready their organizations to execute. Jonathan Akers illustrated the difference between these two approaches when he drove a high-stakes decision at a multinational software company.

Jonathan Akers had recently landed a global role as vice president in corporate planning and was eager to make an impact on the business. The company was entangled in a competitive contest over ownership of the mid-market space. Their largest competitor dominated the small business market, while they owned the enterprise data space. In search of market control and revenue growth, this company began moving down market while their competitor was moving up. Winning the mid market was symbolically important, but it would take an entirely new business model to get there. Jonathan had been asked to lead the development of a new pricing model to enable them to penetrate the market. It was just the opportunity he needed to deliver a tangible success.

Eager to get it right on an issue of such strategic import, Jonathan assembled a team with all the right players, including a broad coalition of leaders from product, marketing, services, and business practices, many of whom had a deep understanding of the mid-market space. The group came together in a large conference room on the top floor of their sleek headquarters in Silicon Valley. Jonathan sat at the head of a narrow table.

He began the conversation by laying out the challenge to the group, teeing up the issues and turning on the heat for the work of the task force. He made it clear that the CEO and the other top lieutenants of the company were expecting significant progress in the mid market. Driven by a high-stakes mandate, people began compiling data and analysis and submitting it to Jonathan over the course of several weeks.

The task force had just been set in motion, but already it was beginning to spin with confusion. Jonathan had left unclear the role the task force members would play and how the recommendations and decisions would actually get made. Instead of using the brainpower inherent in the task force, Jonathan used the task force as an audience for his own ideas. He consumed most of the time of the task force meetings overarticulating his own biases or dropping names. Although he gathered data from each task force member quite tenaciously, none of this information was shared or discussed in the task force meetings. There was plenty of data gathered, but there was simply no debate. The meetings atrophied into opinion-based conversation—mostly Jonathan's. One task force member shared his frustration: "I came to these meetings hoping to hear from this brain trust we assembled, but all I heard was Jonathan's point of view."

Although people were led to believe they would be a critical part of the decision, they quickly realized that the task force wasn't where the decision would be made (or even recommended) nor was it a forum for debate where their individual or collective thinking would be challenged. It appeared that the decision would be made by a select few behind closed doors. The suspicions turned out to be true. Nothing much came of their work, but they did eventually receive a sudden e-mail from Jonathan with the subject line: "Announcement of New Pricing Model" and knew the decision had been made without them.

Instead of generating collective understanding and optimism about the mid market, Jonathan generated disillusionment about the company's prospects for winning in this market, and he personally earned a reputation as a time waster. The immediate impact was apparent the next time Jonathan called a task force meeting: every other chair around the huge conference room table was empty. But the more far-reaching result was that the company continued to stall in the mid market while their competitors gained traction and market share.

This is a story played out far beyond this top floor conference room. It is repeated because, while many leaders like Jonathan attempt the management practice of inclusion and discussion, they are still operating with an elitist view of intelligence, believing the brainpower for the organization sits with a select few. They lack a rich view of intelligence in which there are many sources of insight waiting to be more fully utilized and where intelligence actually develops through engagement and challenge.

A leader's ability to garner the full intelligence of the organization depends on some of his or her most deeply held assumptions.

THE DECISION MAKER VERSUS THE DEBATE MAKER

Mind of the Multiplier

Diminishers like Jonathan Akers seem to hold an assumption that *there are only a few people worth listening to*. Sometimes they state that thought out loud, like the executive who admitted to listening to only one or two people from his 4,000-person organization. But typically such executives manifest their assumption in more subtle ways. They ask their direct reports to interview candidates for an open position but they end up hiring the person their "star employee" favors. They say they have an open-door policy, but seem to spend a lot of time in closed-door meetings with one or two highly influential advisors. They might patronize people by asking for their opinion, but when it comes down to the high-stakes decisions, they make them privately and announce them to the organization.

Multipliers hold a very different view. They don't focus on what they know but on how to know what others know. They seem to assume that *with enough minds we can figure it out*. They are interested in every relevant insight people can offer. Like the executive who even late at night, after a twelve-hour debate, insisted the team listen to one more comment from a junior member of the group. The comment turned out to be the crucial insight necessary for solving the question at hand. It's no surprise that Multipliers approach decisions by bringing people together, discovering what they know, and encouraging people to challenge and stretch each other's thinking through collective dialogue and debate.

These core assumptions lie at the heart of the differences in how Diminishers and Multipliers make decisions. By assuming there are only a few people worth listening to, Diminishers operate as Decision Makers: when the stakes are at their highest, they rely on their own knowledge or an inner circle of people to make the decision.

When Multipliers are faced with a high-stakes decision, they have a different gravity pull toward the full brainpower of their organization. In harnessing this knowledge, they play the role of the Debate Maker. They realize that not all decisions need collective input and debate, but on decisions of consequence, they lead rigorous debate that prosecutes the issues with hard facts and depersonalizes decisions. Through debate, they challenge and stretch what people know, thus making the organization smarter over time and creating the organizational will to execute the decisions made.

The Decider vs. a Team of Rivals

Examining the core decision-making approach of President George W. Bush and President Barack Obama reveals key differences in their stated approach to making high-stakes decisions.

Mr. Bush has characterized himself as "the decider."[1] And *Time* magazine[2] described him as leading "The Blink Presidency," after Malcolm Gladwell's book *Blink* about the phenomenon of making instantaneous decisions.

In an interview with *Washington Post* writer Bob Woodward, Mr. Bush said, "I'm a gut player. I play by instincts. I don't play by the book." After writing a four-book series on the President, which included eleven hours of personal interviews with Mr. Bush, Woodward concluded, "I think [Bush] is impatient. I think, my summation: He doesn't like homework. And homework means reading or getting briefed or having a debate. And part of the presidency, part of governing, particularly in this area, is homework, homework, homework."

We saw the consequences of rapid, centralized decision making, which led the United States into war with Iraq in 2003. Regarding the 2007 surge in Iraq, Mr. Bush asked tougher questions of his security team than he had with the original invasion because "Different times call for different kinds of questions."[3] But as a matter of record, he kept himself away from some of the meetings where key decisions about the surge were made, telling Woodward, "I'm not in these meetings, you'll be happy to hear, because I got other things to do."

In contrast, Mr. Obama has stated an intent to follow Abraham Lincoln's approach to decision making. An approach that can be summarized by the title of a book by Doris Kearns Goodwin on Lincoln called *A Team of Rivals*. After introducing members of his national security team at a press conference in December 2008, which included his fierce rival in the election primaries, Hillary Clinton, as secretary of state, Mr. Obama was asked how he would ensure the group worked as a team of rivals rather than a clash of rivals. He responded with clarity:

I assembled this team because I am a strong believer in strong per-
sonalities and strong opinions. I think this is how the best decisions
are made. One of the dangers in a White House, based on my reading
of history, is that you get wrapped up in group think and everybody
agrees with everything and there is no discussion and no dissenting
views. So I am going to be welcoming a vigorous debate inside the
White House. Understand that I will be setting policy as President.
I will be responsible for the vision that this team carries out, and I
expect them to implement that vision once decisions are made.

According to a *New York Times* article on March 28, 2009, Mr.
Obama's stated approach to foreign policy decisions has been carried
out in practice. The article outlines the debate that took place in the
White House over the plan to widen the efforts being made in the
Afghanistan war. "The debate over the past few weeks," wrote Helene
Cooper, "offered a glimpse into how Mr. Obama makes decisions." In
the end, a compromise was reached that "reflected all the strains of the
discussion among his advisers."

David Brooks wrote about Obama's approach to foreign policy decision making this way:

The election revolved around passionate rallies. The Obama
White House revolves around a culture of debate. He leads long,
analytic discussions, which bring competing arguments to the
fore. He sometimes seems to preside over the arguments like a
judge settling a lawsuit.

His policies are often a balance as he tries to accommodate dif-
ferent points of view. He doesn't generally issue edicts. . . . This
style has never been more evident than in his decision to expand
the war in Afghanistan.[4]

These two approaches capture the essence of the difference between
Decision Makers and Debate Makers. History will show the long-term

impact of these two approaches, but even in matters of high politics, the approach a leader takes in making a decision matters.

THE DEBATE MAKER

Lutz Ziob, the executive at Microsoft highlighted earlier, approaches decision making in his organization with both the mind and the practices of a Debate Maker. When Lutz took over the education business at Microsoft in 2003, it was a traditional education business that delivered five-day instructor-led classes through corporate training partners. But it was falling short of its goals for revenue and reach.

Lutz faced a double whammy: the organization urgently needed to return to positive and profitable revenue growth, and at the same time, it needed to greatly extend its reach to ensure as many customers and potential customers as possible had a command of Microsoft's technology. As general manager of the Microsoft Learning Business, Lutz needed to decide if they should look for this revenue and reach within the current base of corporate training partners or if they should pursue a bold—and potentially risky—new approach in the academic sector.

Lutz, who speaks with a softened German accent, has that rare combination of passion and reserve. He is a veteran of the technology education business, with a masterful command of both the strategy and the details of running his business. His team is diverse, precisely because he has recruited them to be. Several are longtime Microsoft staffers. Others have deep experience with education at other global technology firms. Several are new to their current role, because they are in stretch assignments outside their usual domain and functional expertise.

After fifteen minutes with Lutz, you can tell he is quite capable of making these decisions himself, given his vast knowledge. And given the stakes, many executives would have felt the pull to do so. But Lutz has a bias for debate and a conviction that the more vital the decision, the more rigorous and inclusive the decision-making process should be. So he set out to engage his leadership team with the challenge at hand.

He gathered his team and teed up the issue with a big question: Should they refocus their entire business on the academic market, distributing education through the schools instead of through corporate training providers? Should they risk their current business model to potentially achieve significantly higher reach? He gave the team their assignments. They would meet in a couple of weeks on Orcas Island near Microsoft's HQ in Redmond, Washington. They were to bring all the information they could gather and come with views about the academic market space.

Gathered on Orcas Island, the team had the usual offsite environment—a great physical location, pens and flip charts, a big, open, light conference room—but more important, they had been given permission to think! Because everyone was prepared, Lutz could quickly frame the issue and launch right into the challenge: "As you know, the entire $300 million education business we are in has been based on a potentially outdated model. The decision we face is whether to cling to this business model or introduce a totally new model that would push the education out of the corporate classroom space and into academics where we would reach students much earlier in their careers."

He set broad parameters for the debates. He insisted, "I expect your best thinking here. Everyone should feel not only welcome to speak up, but an obligation to speak up. You can expect us to be thorough. We will be prosecuting assumptions and asking ourselves the tough questions." Then he officially launched the first of several debates.

He sparked the debate through a series of bold questions: "Should we be in the academic space?" and "What would success require?" After each question, he let the team jump in, and he let the debate proceed.

As the discussion was beginning to reach a settling point, he pushed harder, asking people to switch sides and argue against their previously stated position. He chimed in, "Chris, switch sides with Raza.

Raza, you've been for this idea, you now argue against it. Chris, you now argue for it." They would switch roles, which felt awkward for a moment or two, but soon they'd begin to pound the issues from the other vantage point. Or to broaden people's perspectives, he asked his people to assume roles outside of their functional area. Lutz persisted, "Teresa, you've been offering an international perspective on this, now look at it with a domestic hat on." And "Lee Anne, you've been look-ing at the technical issues. I want you to debate this from the market-ing perspective." The team stepped away from their positions and a new set of sparks erupted. Lutz loved to stir up controversy and would become noticeably disappointed if the debate wasn't charged and the sparks weren't flying.

The team listened passionately to the rich and different perspec-tives. They challenged one another's assumptions and often their own. They happily dropped the polite professionalism that typifies so many corporate meetings and took on the challenges with an almost ferocious appetite. This was a high-stakes approach to a high-stakes decision.

In the end, the organization decided that they would pursue the academic market, and they spent the next two years repivoting the business around students and academia. The business expanded their reach from 1,500 corporate training partners to 4,700 academic partners—three times the scale in just two years. It is currently set to become the biggest reach driver of their now-profitable business.

Lutz did not leave debate to chance. He knew that while creat-ing a debate is easy, creating a rigorous debate requires a deliberate approach.

THE THREE PRACTICES OF THE DEBATE MAKER

In our research we found that Multipliers did three specific things very differently from Diminishers when it came to decision making.

While Diminishers raise issues, dominate discussions, and force decisions, Multipliers: 1) frame the issues; 2) spark the debate; and 3) drive sound decisions. Let us examine each of these in more detail.

I. Frame the Issue

Our research showed that Debate Makers know that the secret sauce of a great debate is what they do *before* the debate actually begins. They prepare the organization for the debate by forming the right questions and the right team and framing the issues and process in a way in which everyone can contribute. The process is broken down below.

Define the Question

Tim Brown, the chief executive and president of IDEO, the famously innovative global design consultancy firm, said:

> As leaders, probably the most important role we can play is asking the right questions and focusing on the right problems. It's very easy in business to get sucked into being reactive to the problems and questions that are right in front of you. It doesn't matter how creative you are as a leader, it doesn't matter how good the answers you come up with. If you're focusing on the wrong questions, you're not really providing the leadership you should.[5]

Multipliers use their own know-how to shape the way people look at issues. They have the ability to frame the questions in a way that nobody else would have thought about. They sift through a variety of factors to identify the right issues and spend time formulating the right questions. These questions:

- Unearth and challenge the assumptions that entrench the organization in old patterns and thinking;

- Surface the fundamental tensions and tradeoffs to be considered in a decision;

- Force people to examine the facts and confront reality;

- Ensure multiple perspectives on an issue.

As Tim Brown said, "The right questions aren't just kind of lying around on the ground to be picked up and asked."[6] The work of the Multiplier is to find the right issue and formulate the right question, so others can find the answers.

Form the Team

Multipliers ensure a great debate by having the right people in the debate. Potential candidates for a great debate include:

- Those with knowledge or insight needed to inform the issue

- Key stakeholders for the decision

- Those with responsibility for driving the outcome of the decision

Assemble the Data

Multipliers identify the decision-critical data that needs to be gathered and analyzed prior to the debate. They ask others to come to the debate armed with relevant information so they are prepared to contribute. When Tim Cook, the COO of Apple Inc., assembles a team to debate an important business decision, the team knows they are expected to gather and thoroughly analyze the data in advance. Tim's team understands that when they offer their opinions, those opinions need to be informed by fact, not anecdote. One member of Tim's management team is known for bringing in a box of extra backup data with him to these debates—just in case.

Frame the Decision

In preparation for the meeting itself, Debate Makers define what needs to be addressed, why it is important, and how the final decision is expected to be made.

The What. Multipliers explicitly state what question needs to be addressed.

The Why. They shed light on what is happening in the environment that is prompting the need for the debate, and they lay out the stakes involved.

The How. Multipliers take time up front to clarify the decision-making process and establish roles, including their own. They answer questions such as:

■ How long will we have to make the decision?

■ Who will recommend?

■ Who will decide?

As a result of properly framing the issues, every person knows what is at stake, what is expected of them, and the level of honesty and rigor that will be required of the group as a whole.

In illustrating how Debate Makers frame the issues, let's return to Lutz at Microsoft. Recently Lutz needed to make a tough budget cut decision, so he pulled his lieutenants together for a debate. According to a member of his management team, "He teed up the issue and set the context for the meeting: 'We are here to answer a tough question: What is the best way to take 20 percent out of our budget?'" He went on to explain the need for action. He was fully transparent. He didn't hoard information. He just shared openly that HQ had requested a certain amount of budget back and why. Then he outlined the process: each person needed to explain where the money should be taken out of the organization and why. Once it was debated fully, he would make the final decision. They debated for more than two hours, during which time he played the role of facilitator, ensuring that each member of his team debated the issues rigorously.

When a decision is high stakes, Debate Makers require everyone's best thinking. They know people will do their best thinking if the issues are framed well and defined, and the questions of the debate are clear. They know that the debate will be richest if it is based in facts, not opinions, and that it takes foresight to gather the right information.

Because they take time to prepare and frame the issue, Multipliers are able to leverage more capability from their people than their Diminisher counterparts. Multipliers ensure people don't waste their brainpower and enthusiasm "spinning" on tangential issues. By framing the debate in terms of key questions within a clear context, they are able to foster motivation and readiness and help elicit 100 percent from their people. Multipliers love debate, but they debate with a purpose. They know what they want out of the debate and what they want out of the people involved. Multipliers aren't just debaters; they are Debate Makers.

II. Spark the Debate

After framing of the issue, Multipliers spark the debate. Through our research and coaching work with executives, I have observed four elements of a great debate. A great debate is:

- *Engaging:* The question is compelling and important to everyone in attendance.

- *Comprehensive:* The right information is shared to generate a holistic and collective understanding of the issues at hand.

- *Fact based:* The debate is deeply rooted in fact, not opinion.

- *Educational:* People leave the debate more focused on what they learned than on who won or lost.

How do you lead this type of debate? There are two key elements that couple and form the yin and the yang of great debate. The first is to create safety. The second is to demand rigor. Multipliers do both.

The Yin: Create Safety for Best Thinking

How do Multipliers create a safe climate for people's best thinking?

They do it by removing fear. They remove the factors that cause people to doubt themselves or their ideas and the fear that causes people to hold back. One senior manager we interviewed told us about his current boss, "Amit has strong opinions but he lets the discussion happen *before* he expresses that opinion." And further, "You know where you stand with Amit. He maintains a balance of respect but is also brutally honest if something doesn't make sense. I've never gotten into trouble telling my manager what I think."

Another executive we've worked with knew that she had a reputation for being smart and strong willed, and that she could be intimidating. A direct report has noticed a recent change in her: "When the group is debating an issue, Jennifer makes it a point to hold her views until the end. She gives a chance for each member of her executive team to express his or her views before she adds her own."

Multipliers create safety, but they also maintain pressure for a reality-based, rigorous debate. Multipliers make sure everyone is wearing a seat belt because they are about to put their foot on the accelerator.

The Yang: Demand Rigor

How do Multipliers demand rigor?

They ask the questions that challenge conventional thinking. They ask the questions that unearth the assumptions that are holding the organization back. They ask the questions that cause the team to think harder and to dig deeper.

They ask for evidence. They aren't overly swayed by opinion and emotional arguments; they continue to ask for evidence that would confirm a point of view. And they ask for evidence that might suggest an alternative point of view.

They pursue all sides of the issue. When the group moves too quickly toward agreement, Multipliers often step back and ask someone to argue the other point of view. Or they might make the argument themselves. They make sure all the rocks are turned over.

When the senior management team of a European online distribution company met to discuss whether to add a new feature to their online store, there was strong support for the idea among the team. But the CEO wasn't satisfied with intuition and wanted to drive more rigor into their collective thinking. He asked the senior executive team whether the new feature would actually drive higher sales. At first there were opinions, but the CEO wanted data and wanted to know what the facts proved. The executive team began to dig into the facts in a summary analysis. Again the CEO dug deeper. He asked the group to go country by country, poring over the data to look for an answer to the questions.

As one executive who was present said, "Nobody got away with their own opinions." The group wrestled with the issue until they finally concluded that they didn't have enough information yet to make a clear decision, and they identified what additional data they needed. This company's leader kept the debate going by demanding rigor and sound decision making.

According to one of his management team members, Jim Barksdale, former CEO of Netscape, was well known for saying, "If you don't have any facts, we'll just use my opinion."

Sue Siegel, as president of Affymetrix, led the company through a moment-of-truth decision in 2001 by using the power of facts and openness to harness the full brainpower of the organization.

Affymetrix produced microarray technologies that allow scientists to analyze complex genetic information. The company had been public for three years and had grown steadily to 800 employees. Sue received some troubling news from customers that there were some problems with the GeneChip microarrays that could potentially render inaccurate results, but only for a minor portion of its applications. As president, she would have to make one of the toughest decisions that the company would face in the next several years: should they recall the product?

Sue was herself a veteran executive of the life sciences industry and had deep knowledge of the underlying technology and issues. But instead of relying solely on her own understanding of the situation, she went beyond the management hierarchy and reached deep into the organization for data and for insight. She went straight to the people who understood the issues and let them know she needed their input.

She then convened a larger forum of several layers and management. She framed the magnitude of the issue and the potential impact to the company. She laid out a couple scenarios and then began asking questions. She ensured that the group thought through the decision from every angle: "What is the impact on our customers? . . . What is our legal obligation? . . . What is the financial impact?" Sue asked for data and their recommendations. The group then debated for two arduous days. After several debates, she asked the management team to weigh in, and then they made the decision to recall the product. The next day, Sue boarded a plane to present at the Goldman Sachs financial conference in Laguna Niguel attended by over 1,000 analysts, shareholders, and industry experts to tell them about their mistake and their decision.

The product recall was a financial setback for the young organization, adversely impacting market cap for two quarters and sending it from Wall Street darling to leper overnight. However, with the company staff behind the decision, they were able to execute the decision with conviction and explain it to their customers and to the market. This allowed them to rebound quickly to regain their market position and exceed their market cap. In fact, the product recall became a turning point in building deep customer relationships and respect for employee input that would become the hallmark of the company. In the four years that Sue led the company following the product recall, Affymetrix continued to grow sales and beat expectations for both revenue and earnings.

Sue Siegel led this organization successfully through one of its toughest decisions because instead of turning inward, she reached out and utilized the full intelligence of the organization to make a decision that was grounded in full disclosure and fact, and in the best interest of their customers.

The following chart summarizes some of the practices Debate Makers use to create safety while also demanding rigor:

CREATE SAFETY FOR BEST THINKING (THE YIN)	■ Share their view last after hearing other people's views ■ Encourage others to take an opposing stand ■ Encourage all points of view ■ Focus on the facts ■ Depersonalize the issues and keep it unemotional ■ Look beyond organizational hierarchy and job titles
DEMAND RIGOR (THE YANG)	■ Ask the hard questions ■ Challenge the underlying assumptions ■ Look for evidence in the data ■ Attack the issues, not the people ■ Ask "why" repeatedly until the root cause is unearthed ■ Equally debate both sides of the issue

III. Drive a Sound Decision

Multipliers may relish a great debate, but they pursue debate with a clear end: a sound decision. They ensure this in three ways. First, they reclarify the decision-making process. Second, they make the decision or explicitly delegate it to someone else to decide. And third, they communicate the decision and the rationale behind it.

Reclarify the Decision-Making Process

After the issue has been debated, Multipliers let people know the next step in the decision-making process. They summarize the key ideas and outcomes of the debate, and they let people know what to expect next. They address such questions as:

- Are we making the decision right now or do we need more information?

- Is this a team decision or will the leader make the final call?

- If it is a team decision, how will we resolve any differing views?

- Has anything that has surfaced in the debate altered the decision-making process?

One executive we studied was strong on closure: "Allison says who is going to make the decision and when. People aren't left in limbo wondering how the decision will be made."

Multipliers let people know what will be done with their thinking and their work. With this sense of closure, people around them are assured that their discretionary effort won't be wasted, and they are likely to give 100 percent the next time. In this way Multipliers get full contribution not just once, but over and over again.

Make the Decision

Although Multipliers know how to generate and leverage collective thinking, they are not necessarily consensus-oriented leaders. At times, they may seek the full consensus of the group; however, our research shows that they are equally comfortable making the final decision.

One manager responsible for emerging markets within a global technology firm said of her leader, "Chris prefers collective decisions and consensus, but he's practical and he'll either make the final decision for speed or defer to someone else because it is clearly within that person's domain."

Communicate the Decision and Rationale

One of the benefits of purposeful, rigorous debate is the business case and momentum it builds to execute the decision. As people debate an issue thoroughly, they develop a deep understanding of the underlying problems and opportunities and the imperatives for change. They put their fingerprint on the decision. Because they achieved a collective understanding, they are capable of executing collectively.

Lutz often held his organization's debates in a conference room they came to call "The Theater." The Theater looked like any other conference room, with a large conference table that the key players sat at during the debates. However, the room had twice as many chairs set up around the perimeter of the room. These debates were open to anyone in the organization. Anyone interested in the issue could come and listen. The team called it The Theater because it was like a surgical theater in a teaching hospital. As people watched these debates, they came to a better understanding of the issues. When decisions were reached, there were people at all levels of the organization ready to execute. With this model of transparent decision making, communicating the decision and the rationale is easy because the organization is already prepared to move forward.

The Theater not only helped employees in this organization understand and prepare to execute the decision at hand; they were also learning what was expected of them when they were called to the table to a debate on another issue. They were like medical students learning to perform surgery.

THE DIMINISHER'S APPROACH TO DEBATE

Instead of looking out broadly into their organization for intelligence, Diminishers tend to make decisions quickly either based solely on their own opinions or with input from a close inner circle. Then people begin to spin and speculate and get distracted from enthusiastically carrying the decisions out.

In sharp contrast to The Theater of the executive above, one Diminisher I worked with held meetings in his office in a two-circle format. Seated at a small, round table was his equally small inner circle, who would discuss the issue and make the decisions. But around the perimeter of the room was a collection of silent people standing and taking notes. After participating in this strange meeting format, I couldn't help but ask one of these voiceless individuals standing on the outer edge about the role of this silent body. She said, "Oh, we don't ever participate in these decisions and we certainly don't get a 'seat at the table.' We're just here to take notes so our SVP doesn't have to tell us what to do later." This was less of a surgical theater and more of a lecture auditorium.

Instead of framing issues for debate and decisions, Diminishers tend to raise issues abruptly, then dominate the discussion before forcing a decision.

RAISE ISSUES. When a problem surfaces, Diminishers bring issues or decisions to people's attention, but they don't necessarily frame them in a way that allows others to easily contribute. When they raise the issue, they focus on the "what" rather than on the "how" or the "why" of a decision. One CIO routinely raised a variety of distracting issues at his weekly staff meetings. One of his directors explained, "Once he came in and raised the issue of ergonomically sound keyboards and then went on about them for an hour. He is intense and intelligent, but all over the place. He makes a millimeter of progress in a million directions."

DOMINATE THE DISCUSSION. When issues get discussed or debated, Diminishers tend to dominate the discussion with their own ideas. They are debaters, not Debate Makers. Looking back at Jonathan Akers, where did he fall short? He gathered the right players and he gathered the data. But he never sparked a debate. Instead he dominated the discussions with his opinions and shut down the intelligence—and drive—of the players he had assembled.

FORCE THE DECISION. Rather than driving a sound decision, Diminishers tend to force a decision. They force the decision either by relying heavily on their own opinion or by short-cutting a rigorous debate. As one executive said in an attempt to drive closure after dominating the discussion during a task force meeting, "I think we're all in agreement that we should centralize this function on a global level." The group looked bewildered, knowing that this was not the shared opinion of the group. One brave woman broke the silence and responded with, "No, Joe, we have heard your opinion, but we don't have agreement."

What is the impact to the organization of the Diminisher's approach to decision making? At first glance, it appears that Diminishers make efficient decisions. However, because their approach only utilizes the intelligence of a small number of people and ignores the rigor of debate, the broader organization is left in the dark, not understanding the decision, nor the assumptions and facts upon which it is based. With this lack of clarity, people turn to debating the soundness of a decision rather than executing it.

This spin phenomenon is one of the reasons Diminishers create resource drain rather than resource leverage.

DEBATE MAKING AS RESOURCE LEVERAGE

Multipliers don't act as Debate Makers because it makes people feel good. Multipliers operate as Debate Makers because they want to leverage every ounce of intelligence and capability they can in making and executing sound decisions.

The following chart reflects why Decision Makers leave capability on the table while Debate Makers leverage and stretch the capability of their resources:

Decision Makers		Debate Makers	
What They Do	*What They Get*	*What They Do*	*What They Get*
Engage a select inner circle in the decision-making process	Underutilization of the bulk of their resources, while a select few are overworked A lack of information from those closest to the action, resulting in poorer decisions Too many resources thrown at those who don't have the understanding they need to execute the decisions effectively	Access a wide spectrum of thinking in a rigorous debate before making decisions	High utilization of the bulk of their resources Real information they need to make sound decisions Efficient execution with lower resource levels because they have built a deep understanding of the issues, which readies the organization to execute

In summary, Decision Makers don't use the full complement of talent, intelligence, and information that is available to them. This capacity sits idle in their organization. To counteract this, they continue to ask the organization for more resources, wondering why they aren't more productive.

In contrast to this, Multipliers not only engage the best thinking of the resources around them; they use debate to stretch the thinking of the individuals and the team. While decisions are debated vigorously, real facts and issues surface, forcing people to listen and learn. As a result, Multipliers get full capability out of their current resources and they stretch and increase the capacity of the organization to take on the next challenge.

This begs a question: how does someone learn to lead debate like Lutz at Microsoft Learning or Sue Siegel at Affymetrix? How does someone go from being a Decision Maker to a Debate Maker?

BECOMING A DEBATE MAKER

Our research and experience coaching executives reveals that leaders can move along the Diminisher–Multiplier continuum. But it requires more than just adding some new leadership practices. It often requires a fundamental shift in the assumptions of the leader. Often this shift happens when a leader begins to view his or her role differently. It can happen when leaders see that their greatest contribution lies in asking the questions that produce the most rigorous thinking and answers.

Several years ago I volunteered to be a discussion leader for a Junior Great Books program at an elementary school. It seemed like a simple volunteer job. The assignment was straightforward: lead a discussion of a group of third-grade students on a piece of great youth literature. The goal was clear: have them dig deep into the story for meaning and debate it with their peers. Despite my protests that I knew how to facilitate discussion, I was sent to a one-day training workshop to learn a technique called "shared inquiry."[7] What I found was a simple but powerful technique for leading debate.

There are three rules to shared inquiry:

1. The discussion leader only asks questions. This means that the leader isn't allowed to answer his or her questions or give his or her interpretation of the story's meaning. This keeps the students from relying on the leader's answers.

2. The students must supply evidence to support their theories. If the student thinks that Jack went up the beanstalk a third time to prove his invincibility, he or she is required to identify a passage (or more than one) in the text that supports this idea.

3. Everyone participates. The role of the leader is to make sure everyone gets airtime during the discussion. Often the leader needs to restrain stronger voices and proactively call on the more timid voices.

As a discussion leader, it was liberating to ask the questions but not give the answers. In fact, I found it strangely powerful. And when the students spouted off their views and interpretations of the story, it was thrilling to look them straight in the eye and say, "Do you have any evidence to support that claim?" Initially, they looked terrified. But they quickly learned that the cost of an opinion was evidence. As they gained experience, they learned to respond quickly. They would assert an opinion, and then I would insist (with my best intimidating look), "Show me your evidence." They would scurry to locate the exact place in the text that supported their claim and cite it with conviction. And because everyone was called on, every student learned to state their views and support their ideas with data.

This experience cemented my belief that there is a process and a formula for great debate.

The Starting Block

We've gone through a master approach to how Multipliers create debate, but here is a simplified, three-step process to get started:

1. ASK THE HARD QUESTION. Ask the question that will get at the core of the issue and the decision. Ask the question that will confront underlying assumptions. Pose the question to your team and then stop. Instead of following up with your views, hold yours and ask for theirs.

2. ASK FOR THE DATA. When someone offers an opinion, don't let it rest on anecdote. Ask for the evidence. Look for more than one data point. Ask them to identify a cluster of data or a trend. Make it a norm so people come into debates armed with the data—an entire box if necessary.

3. ASK EACH PERSON. Reach beyond the dominant voices to gather in and hear all views and all data. You might find that the softer voices belong to the analytical minds who are often most familiar with and objective about the data.

As you rethink your role as a leader, you will come to see that your greatest contribution might depend on your ability to ask the right question, not have the right answer. You will see that all great thinking starts with a provocative question and a rich debate, whether it is in the mind of one person or an entire community.

DISCUSSION, DISSENT, AND DEBATE

Hubert H. Humphrey, America's vice president under Lyndon B. Johnson, captured the essential principle of how Multipliers make decisions when he said: "Freedom is hammered out on the anvil of discussion, dissent, and debate." Our research showed that it is this discussion, dissent, and debate that also hammers out sound decisions. Intelligence Multipliers know how to create this debate to generate strong support for high-stakes decisions while also building the collective muscle of the organization to deliver on promised results.

THE MULTIPLIER FORMULA

THE DECISION MAKER VERSUS THE DEBATE MAKER

DECISION MAKERS decide efficiently with a small inner circle, but they leave the broader organization in the dark to debate the soundness of the decision instead of executing it.

DEBATE MAKERS engage people in debating the issues up front, which leads to sound decisions that people understand and can execute efficiently.

The Three Practices of the Debate Maker

1. *Frame the Issue*
   - Define the question
   - Form the team
   - Assemble the data
   - Frame the decision

2. *Spark the Debate*
   - Create safety for best thinking
   - Demand rigor

3. *Drive a Sound Decision*
   - Reclarify the decision-making process
   - Make the decision
   - Communicate the decision and rationale

Becoming a Debate Maker

1. Ask the hard question
2. Ask for the data
3. Ask each person

Unexpected Findings

1. As a leader, you can have a very strong opinion but also facilitate debate that creates room for other people's views. Data is the key.

2. Debate Makers are equally comfortable being the decision maker in the end. They are not only consensus-driven leaders.

3. Rigorous debate doesn't break down a team; it builds them and makes the team stronger.

CHAPTER 6

THE INVESTOR

If you want to build a ship, don't drum up the men to
gather wood, divide the work and give orders. Instead,
teach them to yearn for the vast and endless sea.

ANTOINE DE ST. EXUPERY

It is after midnight at the McKinsey office in Seoul, South Korea. The lights are out, except in one conference room occupied by a project team that is two days away from a critical presentation to one of the firm's biggest clients in Asia. The team is led by Hyunjee, a sharp, highly regarded project leader. Joining them this night is Jae Choi, one of McKinsey's Seoul-based partners. Jae knows the team has a critical deadline and, as is typical, is meeting with the team to guide, challenge, and shape the thinking as they build the first major presentation of their findings to the client.

The project leader, Hyunjee, is at the whiteboard. She and the team are retesting the story line with some new facts that surfaced during the past week. The team is struggling to integrate the findings into the overarching message about the client's business transformation. Jae listens carefully and asks a lot of questions, as he is known to do.

It becomes clear that the team is stuck. The team leader is systematically working this tough problem, but looks at Jae with that desperate look that signals, "I could use a little help here!" Jae has been on countless numbers of these projects and has stood in the project leader's shoes many times. He can see a story line that the team, who has been buried in the details, has not yet considered.

Jae offers a few thoughts for the team to discuss, standing up to take the whiteboard marker from the team leader. Heading to the board, he begins to list several emerging themes, encouraging the team to view the facts from a different angle. The group is thrilled to have this fresh perspective, and excited voices are now engaged in testing, pushing, and building on the ideas despite the late hour. With the new insights coming from the renewed discussions, Jae can now visualize the new presentation flow in his mind. He feels a familiar comfort up at the whiteboard. The desire to drive the team toward completion is alluring. He is tempted to lay it all out for the team so they can all go home and get some rest. The consultant in Jae tells him to go on and finish the job and complete the story line himself. But the leader in Jae signals restraint. He stops sketching and turns to the project leader, checking to see if she is comfortable with the new direction. Seeing the smile on her face, Jae says, "Okay . . . looks like we've got a new line of thinking to run with. Let's see what you can do with this." He then hands the pen back to Hyunjee, who resumes command of the process and leads the team to build an outstanding presentation for the client.

Surely it was tempting for Jae to jump in, rescue the struggling team, and drive the presentation to completion himself. He would have felt like a hero (and probably a few years younger, too). And it was appealing for the team to let him do it, given the late hour. But Jae's proclivity to invest in people and their development won out. Jae reflected on the leader's role: "You can jump in and teach and coach, but then you have to give the pen back. When you give that pen back, your people know they are still in charge."

When something is off the rails, do you take over or do you invest? When you take the pen to add your ideas, do you give it back? Or does it stay in your pocket?

Multipliers invest in the success of others. They may jump in to teach and share their ideas, but they always return to accountability.

When leaders fail to return ownership, they create dependent organizations. This is the way of the Diminisher. They jump in, save the day, and drive results through their personal involvement. When leaders return the pen, they cement the accountability for action where it should be. This creates organizations that are free from the nagging need of the leader's rescue.

Multipliers enable others to operate independently by giving other people ownership for results and investing in their success. Multipliers can't always be present to perform emergency rescues, so they ensure people on their teams are self-sufficient and can operate without their direct presence.

Thus far the book has explored why Multipliers make people smarter and more capable in their presence. But now I ask you to consider a different question: What happens when the Multiplier isn't there? What happens to people when the sunlight of the Multiplier isn't shining in their part of the world? This chapter addresses this most curious question: Can Multipliers create an organization that can act intelligently and deliver results without their direct involvement?

THE MICROMANAGER VERSUS THE INVESTOR

Multipliers operate as Investors. They invest by infusing others with the resources and ownership they need to produce results independent of the leader. It isn't just benevolence. They invest, and they expect results.

Forever Strong

Larry Gelwix stood on the side of the rugby pitch, watching his high school team practice. He thought back to the first team he had coached to the national championships. He remembered them being up before dawn, training together. Larry said under his breath, "Well, that was then."

The team in front of him was good, to be sure. They were learning the game, but he noticed they didn't have the physical stamina of previous teams. Larry felt stuck. It wasn't like he hadn't tried. He reminded them at practice all the time. They would nod their heads, but then they didn't do it.

He could cancel practices and hold fitness training in its place, but that risked the skill level of the team. He could yell at them, but that would only work for a day or two. Larry leaned over to an associate coach and said, "We need to turn this over to the captains!"

The next day, Larry stood up, walked quickly to the chalkboard, and drew a line from one side of the board to the other. He said, "We have six weeks left until the finals, and it takes a pretty good athlete six or seven weeks to build the endurance he needs." The coaches and captains were listening to every word. He continued, "If we figure this out now, we can win the Nationals. If we can't, we'll be running on empty."

Larry said, "There are two options: the coaches can keep trying to figure something out or you as the captains can take ownership for finding a solution. What should we do?"

There was a pause. Then the captain of the backs said, "We'll take it on."

Larry said, "Right now I own this challenge. Once you take it on, you'll own it completely. We'll expect an update from you two weeks from today, but we won't bug the team at all."

There was a silent agreement as the captains looked at each other, and the captain of the forwards stood up and went to the board. He turned to Larry who had sat down with the other coaches and said, "Okay, we have a few questions." Larry and the coaches stayed and answered questions about what types of fitness training produced speed, agility, and endurance until, eventually, the coaches were excused and the four captains, all in their teens, stood in a semicircle around the chalkboard figuring it out.

The solution they implemented was to divide the team into small groups of four to six people, each with its own leader. The captains would keep the subgroup leaders accountable, and the leaders would keep the players accountable. The smaller groups met before or after school for fitness training for weeks, and the team soon became one of the fittest in the thirty-four years Larry has coached the team. They went undefeated all season and won the national championship.

How would a micromanaging coach have approached the same problem? We don't need to wonder.

Calling Every Play

Marcus Dolan shouted across the school at John Kimball, "Get over here!" Marcus was a muscle-head coach who wanted to micromanage every aspect of his team. He yelled at one of his team captains, "Don't ever hold a practice without me or you'll be off this team. You've probably already messed everyone up."

Not surprisingly, John didn't try again. He and the other players slowly stopped taking initiative entirely. Playing for Marcus meant you did what he said without question. The endless laps at practice just had to be done. Even in the games, he called every play for every player. The team was so focused and dependent on Marcus, they couldn't think intelligently or adapt rapidly to the changes on the field. They lost every game. Marcus took a group of players that had begun with a sense of ownership for the team and micromanaged it out of them. Interestingly, Marcus Dolan was later elected the most losing coach in high school sports history by *Sports Illustrated*.

More interesting still, eight of his players eventually left the team and went to play for Larry Gelwix. In fact, they were on the team described earlier that woke before dawn to practice. They were the team that led Highland to its first national championship.

Running onto the Field

Why is it that when the stakes are high, so many managers jump in and take over? I've watched hundreds of youth soccer games, and I have to admit that I find myself watching the coaches more than the players (this is one of the curses of genius watching). I've seen a lot of very frustrated coaches during those games when the team is down and playing horribly. I've seen crazy arm waving, copious shouting, and an occasional tantrum on the sideline. But I've never once seen a coach run out onto the field, steal the ball away from a player, drive down the field, and score. It has just never happened. Yet each one of these coaches had the skills required to score the game-winning goal. And I'm sure a few have been tempted to.

So why didn't they? Beyond the obvious reason that it is against the rules, it simply isn't their role. Their job is to coach, and their players' job is to play. What perhaps isn't so obvious is why, when the stakes are high, so many managers in organizations don't hesitate to run onto the playing field, steal away the ball, and score the winning goal. Managers jump in because it isn't illegal, and many can't resist the lure to do so.

- A sales manager who doesn't see fast-enough progress in an important prospective client jumps into the sales process trying to win the deal himself.

- A marketing vice president watches one of her people stumble as he presents the new product go-to-market plan to the CEO, who begins firing tough questions at him. The marketing VP, fearing the CEO will lose confidence in her staff, jumps in and not only answers the tough questions but finishes the presentation.

You might ask yourself: How would I coach if I could never step out on the playing field? How would I lead if I couldn't jump in and take over? How would I respond to a performance gap if I were a Multiplier?

Multipliers understand that their role is to invest, to teach, and to coach, and they keep the accountability for the play with the players. By doing so, they create organizations that can win without them on the field.

Let's now explore the discipline of the Investor and how Multipliers create organizations that can perform and win, not only without them on the field, but long after their direct influence is felt.

THE INVESTOR

Ela Bhatt (or Elaben) is a slight seventy-eight-year-old Indian woman who is soft-spoken to the point of seeming almost fragile. She lives in the simplest two-bedroom bungalow where her bed doubles as a desk chair. She grew up listening to her teachers speak of India's struggle for independence and her parents tell stories of her grandfather joining the twenty-four-day Salt March from Mohandas K. Gandhi's ashram in Ahmedabad to the Arabian Sea to make salt in symbolic defiance of British law.

In order to gain firsthand experience with rural poverty, Elaben went to live in the villages of India and saw for herself that the political independence gained from British rule was not enough. Economic independence would be the next victory. In the villages she saw both the vibrancy and the struggle of the self-employed seamstresses, street vendors, and construction workers and, in response, founded the Self-Employed Women's Association (SEWA) in 1972, which gradually became a significant union in this region.

It would have been easy for Elaben to be elected general secretary of SEWA every three years, as dictated by law, forever. In this way she could have owned the organization's agenda indefinitely and just assigned tasks to everyone else. SEWA, after all, was her creation. It had evolved slowly in her mind and it would have been understandable, if not expected, for her to remain its formal leader in perpetuity.

Yet Elaben insisted on turning over the responsibility for running SEWA to new and younger leadership. She personally invested the time and energy into educating members about the democratic process and encouraged everyone to gain the political literacy needed to step up and run for one of the open positions.

In a fascinating embodiment of SEWA's mission and management philosophy, Jyoti Macwan, who enrolled as a member of SEWA as a poor Guajarati-speaking, cigarette-rolling worker, went on to become the English-speaking general secretary for SEWA. In this role, she has led the union, which at the most recent election involved 1.2 million people. Jyoti could have spent her work years figuring out how to survive from day to day, but because of Elaben's leadership, she has used her intellect solving complex problems that reach across international boundaries and affect more than one million women like herself. She recently stood shoulder to shoulder with Elaben and U.S. Secretary of State Hillary Clinton as they answered questions at a press conference.

Jyoti's story is just the beginning. If you look at the second generation of chief executives of all the SEWA organizations, they all first worked under Elaben's tutelage. Each was given greater and greater ownership as they matured into capable managers.

Every time Elaben established an institution, she invested in the future leaders, which allowed her to step away from the operational management. The succession was handled so gracefully that she could leave with the confidence that her presence would still be felt as she is elsewhere investing her energy in establishing another institution. The SEWA union was followed by a bank (created from 4,000 women each depositing 10 rupees[1]), and this has been followed by the Gujarat Mahila Housing SEWA Trust, the Gujarat State Mahila SEWA Cooperative Federation, SEWA Insurance, SEWA Academy, Homenet South Asia, and many others.

Elaben continues to invest in building leaders and organizations that can operate independently of her. Her influence is like that of a parental figure, giving guidance when people ask for it. She is there when she is needed. Her approach to management is the outgrowth of her simple motto: "A leader is someone who helps others lead."

How does a leader like Elaben create other leaders who can assume ownership and deliver on the mission of the organization themselves? We find answers in the three practices of the Investor.

THE THREE PRACTICES OF THE INVESTOR

As we studied the unique way Multipliers drive results, I found the practices remarkably similar to another world I know. This is a world driven by intellectual assets and investment multiples where technology and business leaders develop other leaders in search of growth and returns and the creation of wealth. This is a world whose nerve center is just a mile from my house.

On Sand Hill Road in Menlo Park, California, home to Silicon Valley's venture capital community, multimillion-dollar investment decisions are made many times daily. Venture capital firms scour industries looking to invest in emerging technologies and young companies destined to become the industry leaders of the future. When a venture firm places its bet and invests a round of funding, it draws up a term sheet to govern the deal. Of particular interest to all parties is the specification of ownership levels. These ownership levels outline relative ownership for the business (postinvestment) and dictate expectations for leadership and for accountability. Simply put, the term sheet lets the parties know who is in charge.

Once ownership of the new company is established, the venture firm cuts a check and the investment of resources begins. This funding provides the financial resources to secure capital, intellectual property, and the human resources to fuel the business. But the value isn't limited to the financial resources. The real value often emerges from the insight and coaching the start-up company receives from the senior partners at the venture firm. These investment partners are men and women who have grown businesses, incubated technology, and often managed very large companies themselves. They not only invest the capital of the fund, they invest their know-how into these nascent companies. They coach the CEO, they lend their Rolodex to assist with business development and sales, and they work with the management team to ensure financial targets can be met.

After infusing capital and know-how, the venture partners look for expected returns. The returns in the marketplace may be years away (or may never materialize), but they watch for key milestones. The accountability is clear. If the company produces expected results, a second or third round of funding is likely. Otherwise the company is left to make it on its own or die on the vine.

Similarly, in their role as Investors, Multipliers define ownership up front and let other people know what is within their charge and what they are expected to build. They invest in the genius of others in a similar way. They teach and coach. They back people up, infusing the resources they need to be successful and to be independent.

And Multipliers complete the same investment cycle as they demand accountability from others. They understand that this accountability isn't ruthless. It is the draw that creates such extraordinary growth of intelligence and capability in others.

We'll look at each of these three steps in turn: 1) define ownership; 2) invest resources; and 3) hold people accountable.

I. Define Ownership

Investors begin this cycle by establishing ownership up front. They see intelligence and capability in the people around them, and they put them in charge.

Name the Lead

When John Chambers, CEO of Cisco, hired his first vice president Doug Allred into the company, he gave the new VP of customer support control and made sure their respective roles were clear. He said, "Doug, when it comes to how we run this area of the company—you get 51 percent of the vote (and you're 100 percent responsible for the result). Keep me in the loop, and consult with me as you go." Weeks later, when Doug was updating John on progress, John responded with, "I knew you'd surprise me on the upside." And it wasn't just Doug who received majority voting rights. John gives "51 percent of the vote" to every member of his management in their respective areas of accountability.

If your boss had told you that you owned 51 percent of the vote, how would you operate? Would you second-guess yourself and run all decisions by him? Or would you swing in the opposite direction and make decisions without consulting him? You probably would do neither. Most likely, you would consult your boss on important decisions to get a second opinion. And on the smaller stuff, you might be wise to ignore him or her as needed to get your job done.

Giving someone 51 percent of the vote and full ownership creates certainty and builds confidence. It enables them to stop second-guessing and start getting second opinions. Clarifying the role that you will play as a leader actually gives people more ownership, not less. They then understand the nature of your involvement and when and how you will invest in their success. And most important, they understand that they hold the majority ownership position and that success or failure hinges on their efforts.

Give Ownership for the End Goal

A management team is assembled for an offsite meeting to plan an important acquisition for their business. They kick off their work with a simple but powerful management exercise called "The Big Picture."[2] The team divides into nine pairs, and each pair is given a one-inch square from a photo of a famous modern painting. Each team is tasked with creating a reproduction and enlargement of its piece of the picture. In other words, each team is given a little piece of a bigger picture. The goal for the team is to bring all the enlargements together to form a unified replica of the original painting. The result should be a painting that is technically accurate and flows together seamlessly. The challenge is that no pair has seen the big picture.

You can imagine what happens first. Each pair, energized by the challenge, studies their one-inch square and begins to replicate it onto the large piece of paper in front of them. They dive into the task, make their sketches, and soon color erupts everywhere. As the time allotted for the first phase of work expires, they start turning their attention to their neighboring colleagues in the room. They begin to connect the pieces and notice that the painting isn't coming together very well. The lines don't match up. The colors don't blend. Their creation is looking like Franken-painting.

The session leader reminds them that their job is to optimize the whole, not their individual piece. They start to pay attention to the bigger picture. They rework their sections, focusing on integration and blending, although it is far too late to create a seamless product. The team delivers the big picture, but it remains a patchwork only moderately resembling the original artwork.

When people are given ownership for only a piece of something larger, they tend to optimize that portion, limiting their thinking to this immediate domain. When people are given ownership for the whole, they stretch their thinking and challenge themselves to go beyond their scope.

When George Schneer, Intel division manager for the EPROM memory chip, was building his management team, he staffed it with leaders from each of the functions in the business value chain: engineering and design, manufacturing, marketing, and sales. These leaders had come from other divisions inside Intel and were accustomed to being measured on the performance of their particular function. The sales leader was measured on sales, the marketing leader on market share, and the manufacturing leader on quality. But George did something different. He asked each member of his management team to assume the same measure of success: profit for the division. The team rallied to ensure the success of the whole division. They managed their individual function, but they readily contributed to solving the challenges in other parts of the business. They offered their full brainpower to the team. Perhaps this is one reason why one member of the management team described the experience this way: "It was our business, and we were winning. There was an exciting pressure. I felt like the smartest guy on the planet."

Stretch the Role

We consistently find that Multipliers get twice the capability from their people that Diminishers do. And time after time, people tell us how Multipliers not only got 100 percent from them, they got 120 percent or even more. Multipliers do get more than 100 percent of people's capability because people grow under the watch of a Multiplier. One way that Multipliers incite this growth is by asking people to stretch and do something they've never done before.

Consider these three individuals:

Eleanor Schaffner Mosh was a champion who needed a bigger cause. As the marketing director for the small IT (information technology) practice inside Booz Allen Hamilton in 1988, she ran basic demand-generation programs. But when Booz decided to turn over the reins of the IT practice to a different partner who was intent on transforming the function, she suddenly found herself with a really big job. Within months she was organizing a corporate-wide kickoff event to launch the vision for the IT practice. Next she convened a forum of the top CIOs in the world. When she found herself sitting next to the CEO of Booz Allen Hamilton during one of these meetings, she confidently explained to him why the IT industry and the IT practice inside their firm was going to change the world. She said, "I wasn't afraid of anything or anyone. We knew what we were doing and we felt like we could do anything."

Mike Hagan was ready to take on the world; but he literally needed a passport. He worked as the director of sales operations for the billion-dollar U.S. sales division of a multinational company. His job was to make sure the sales force complied with company policy. When the president of the sales division wanted to globalize and grow the business, he tapped Mike to figure this out. One day Mike was the policy police, writing tickets for sales administration offenders. The next day he was architecting sales operations and policy for the entire global business. Initially Mike protested, citing his inexperience with global operations. He confessed that he didn't even have a current passport. His protests were ignored. The president told him that he was smart and would surely figure this out. And he did. The experience was grueling but invigorating. Mike reflected, "I was given an opportunity to do something I had never done before. In fact, no one had ever done it." The job was huge, but Mike grew into it as predicted.

Polly Sumner was a powerhouse waiting to be unleashed. When a new president joined Oracle, he noticed this channel sales manager's strategic savvy and drive and asked her to assume a vice president role, running alliances and strategic partnerships. In time, Polly was right in the middle of a very messy high-stakes conflict. The management team could not agree on how quickly Oracle would release new versions of its database code to its applications partner (and also competitor) SAP. Polly escalated the issue to her new boss who responded with, "This is a complex issue, and probably beyond the scope of your role, but you should be the one to lead the resolution." She went right to the people who could fix the problem. She found herself brokering a conversation between the billionaire founders and CEOs, Hasso Plattner of SAP and Larry Ellison of Oracle in a meeting held at Larry's Japanese tea house. The issue was resolved to their mutual satisfaction and Polly was a superstar.

These three individuals all worked for the same boss, just in different settings. Who was the common denominator in this equation? It was Ray Lane, known for challenging his team and for exacting every ounce of their capability. When we asked people why they gave Ray so much, their answers revealed a consistent story: He asked them to do jobs that were far bigger than they were. He could spot smarts in others and gave people a chance to stretch well beyond their current capabilities. He gave them ownership, not at the level of their current capability, but always one—and occasionally two—levels up.

When Investors stretch the role, they stretch the person in it. This bigger role creates a vacuum that must be filled.

II. Invest Resources

The moment Investors establish an ownership position, they step in and begin investing. They protect their investment by infusing the knowledge and resources the person will need to successfully deliver on their accountability.

Teach and Coach

When Jae Choi at McKinsey inserts himself into the discussion with the project team, it isn't to show-and-tell what he knows. He "grabs the pen" so he can teach and coach. It is a simple distinction: Diminishers tell you what they know; Multipliers help you learn what you need to know. Jae is not only a business leader but also an avid teacher who looks for the teachable moments when a team is spinning or has suffered a setback. In these moments, minds are most open and hungry. He contributes a relevant insight or asks just the right question to move the group forward.

K.R. Sridhar, CEO of Bloom Energy, who has been described several times in previous chapters, is another masterful teacher. K.R.'s teaching doesn't occur in a classroom or in a corporate training center. It occurs in the face of very real problems. When the team is wrestling with a technical setback, K.R. engages, not with a solution, but with a thought-provoking question. He asks, "What do we know about what doesn't work?" and "What assumptions led us to these outcomes?" and "What risks do we face now that need to be mitigated?" His team pursues these questions in turn, unearthing their individual knowledge and building a collective body of intelligence.

K.R. says, "You are teaching by helping your team solve real problems. Even if you know the solution, you don't offer it. If you do, you've lost the teaching moment. It has to be Socratic. You ask the question and tease out the answer."

Although K.R. focuses on immediate problems, his investment in these teaching moments returns far more than just solutions to these problems. When leaders teach, they invest in their people's ability to solve and avoid problems in the future. It is one of the most powerful ways that Multipliers build intelligence around them.

Provide Backup

When you think of investing intellectual capital in your direct reports, it is easy to assume that you are the one who needs to provide the capital. But this limits the investment options to what you know and what you have time and energy to invest.

Michael Clarke, the president of a $12 billion division of Flextronics, was facing market consolidation, and he urgently needed to develop an M&A strategy for his business. He had assigned the process of developing that strategy to his very capable vice president of strategy and new ventures, Becky Roller. She worked tirelessly across nine different divisions, pulling together the best of their thinking for a joint two-day strategy session and decision-making forum. But ten days before the event, the entire process was interrupted when they found out an external consulting firm was leading a company-wide strategy initiative that would complicate their M&A strategy and take it in a different direction.

Michael could have jumped in to give extra support, but he suspected he would be more disruptive than helpful. Instead, he asked Greg Keese, his vice president for business development, to work "two-in-a-box" with Becky. He didn't reduce Becky's ownership; Becky was still fully responsible for the project. But given the latest complexities of this project, having two people's perspective and brainpower would be essential. Greg joined Becky for key planning meetings, acted as a sounding board, and offered his support as they navigated the waters. At the completion of the strategy session, Michael praised Becky's leadership and thanked Greg for his backup on this critical project. Watching the management team in action, you could easily imagine the roles reversed next time, with Greg accountable and Becky in the box with him providing backup.

When leaders define clear ownership and invest in others, they have sown the seeds of success and earned the right to hold people accountable.

III. Hold People Accountable

In working with hundreds of business executives, there is something I've noticed about the finest of these leaders. They all appear to have slanted tables in their offices. Sure, the desk they sit at (with their computer and phone) is perfectly flat. But their meeting table has a distinct slant to it. Perhaps you may not have noticed it, but surely you have seen how accountability for action rolls from their side of the table down to other people—and often to you. It may look flat to the unsuspecting eye, but if you placed a marble on one side, that marble would surely roll right off the opposite end! These leaders have a natural leaning to give accountability to others and keep it there. When their people push problems over to the manager's side of the table, by the end of the conversation, those problems slide right back to where they came from. The leader helps, offers suggestions, asks great questions and may escalate a critical issue, but the accountability slides back and rests with their staff. Their tables slant in the direction of other people.

One senior executive I worked for carried a small leather notebook with him in every meeting. Strangely, he never took meeting notes in it. But in every meeting, he was mentally present and fully engaged, listened intently, and offered carefully dispensed insight. During these meetings, I would furiously take notes, making careful notation of my action items. Others did the same. On rare occasions, I would see him write a single note in his book. These occasions were reserved for when he alone was accountable for an action. This was the slanted desk in action. This leader knew how to keep the accountability with his people. He was fully engaged, but he did not take over. And because he assumed accountability with careful restraint, when he wrote an action down in his little leather book, you could be sure it would be done by the next day.

Give It Back

Investors get involved in other people's work, but they continually give back leadership and accountability.

John Wookey is an executive vice president of development at SAP, a veteran of the applications software business and a Multiplier who builds organizations with know-how. He knows that delivering software on time and with quality isn't a hands-off job. But he sees a clear distinction between micromanaging and being involved in the work people are doing.

One of the breeding grounds for micromanagement in the software development business is the user interface review meeting. A typical software application has about 250 screens whose usability can make or break the product in the marketplace, so most executives are keenly interested in getting this right. By the end of a user interface review meeting, the micromanaging development executive will have seized the pen, sprung to the whiteboard, and redesigned the screens himself in front of the group as an impressive show of his design savvy.

John has seen his former peers and bosses do this countless times, but he makes the investment instead. When John sees problems in the screens, he makes suggestions, discusses options and tradeoffs, and then asks the team to go back to their "lab" and figure it out. John says, "I give people feedback as guidance rather than an order because I assume that someone who has been working on something full time, for many weeks, has insight into it that I won't have after a few minutes." John does offer his insights, gained from decades of building business applications, and reminds his team to think about what real users need from the software. He keeps his guidance focused on what they all can do to build a product they can take pride in.

John does jump in but, like the partner at McKinsey in Seoul, he hands the pen back. By doing so, he signals that he is interested and engaged, but he isn't in charge. He gives it back and the accountability for designing and building a great product stays with the other person, who incidentally is also built up in the process.

Michael Clarke, the president of infrastructure at Flextronics, has a clever little two-step process for giving accountability back to people in a way that encourages their continued intellectual contribution. He listens to a presentation or an idea with interest, and then with a wry smile and a thick Yorkshire accent, says, "Hey, that is good thinking." He begins by praising the edge of great thinking. Then he affirms their ownership of the business problem at hand by saying, "I'd love to know whether we should invest in X or Y. I mean, you're smart. You can figure this out." These words are heard again and again by his team: "You're smart. You figure it out." Their ideas are validated and the onus for solving the issue is back with them.

Expect Complete Work

It was the summer of 1987, and I had just landed the internship of my dreams. I would be working for Kerry Patterson, a former professor of organizational behavior at the business school that I attended, who was now running a management training company in Southern California.

Kerry was known for his brilliant but slightly demented mind. Kerry is what happens when you pack an Einstein-size brain into a Danny DeVito–size body. Everyone wanted to work for Kerry, but I managed to get the job through some combination of faculty recommendation and advanced Jedi mind tricks. I eagerly drove to Southern California to work and study under his mentorship.

As in most internships, I did an assortment of odd jobs. I created training content and did computer work and even handled a few stray legal issues. But my favorite job was editing anything that Kerry wrote. Sometimes it was a training manual, sometimes it was a speech, but my job was always to edit and find and fix mistakes. On this particular day, I was editing a marketing brochure that Kerry had written. I did the usual edit. I found and fixed typos and grammar errors. I rewrote a few sentences that were awkward. I then stumbled onto a particularly troublesome tangle of words. I tried a couple times to rewrite the sentences, but I couldn't think of anything better than what Kerry had written. It was too big of a mess for me to fix. I figured Kerry, with his great big brain, would know best how to fix it, so I labeled it as awkward by noting the standard editorial term, "AWK," in the margin. I completed my work and returned the document to Kerry's desk.

About an hour later, Kerry returned from a meeting to find my edits on his desk. I suspected he had read them because I could hear him marching down the hall toward my office. His pace indicated that he wasn't coming to say thank you. He burst across the threshold and marched right up to my desk. Without so much as a "hello," he dropped the document in front of me with a dramatic thump, looked me straight in the eye, and said, "Don't ever give me an A-W-K without an F-I-X!" With a twinkle in his eye, the consummate teacher turned and left my office.

Point taken. I worked a little harder, applied a little more brainpower, and I fixed the awkward sentences. I snuck back into Kerry's office and returned the now-complete edit to his desk. Kerry continued to teach and to write prolifically, and is the author of three best-selling books (*Crucial Conversations*, *Crucial Confrontations*, and *Influencer*). I completed the internship, finished business school, and then made my way in the corporate world having learned from Kerry one of the most important professional lessons: Never give someone an A-W-K without an F-I-X. Don't just identify the problem; find a solution.

Throughout my management career, I've told this story to dozens of people, perhaps hundreds. I've shared it with virtually every person who worked on my team and dropped a problem on my desk without an attached solution. I passed along, "Don't give me an A-W-K without an F-I-X!"

When we ask for the F-I-X, we give people an opportunity to complete their thinking and their work. We encourage them to stretch and exercise intellectual muscles that might otherwise atrophy in the presence of other smart, capable people. Multipliers never do anything for their people that their people can do for themselves.

Respect Natural Consequences

Sarah's dad stood up behind his large desk and said loudly with his Australian accent, "I'm not standing for that!" Sarah had expected him to be disappointed with her choice to skip orchestra practice that day. She was tired of wasting two to three hours of rehearsal when she only had one violin solo at the end. She knew it was mandatory to be at every rehearsal but thought she wouldn't be missed. When they skipped ahead to her part, she wasn't there and the conductor had cut her from the concert. But if Sarah's dad was bothered by her choice to go to the gym, he didn't show it. Instead, he said, "That conductor can't just throw you out. And what are you thinking, just accepting it!" He drove her back to see the conductor.

When they arrived, the conductor emphatically reiterated her position. She said, "Sarah is smart. She knew the rules and made her choice." Sarah's dad tried one tactic after another but he simply didn't have a case. Sarah didn't say a word. She felt foolish standing there. Having her father make excuses made her feel smaller and less capable. She hadn't liked being cut, but she enjoyed being treated like an adult. She preferred being "cut and smart" over being "saved and dumb."

Many corporate managers are like this father. Their well-meaning attempts to help can accidentally diminish people's intelligence and development. They protect people from the natural consequences of their actions, which delays and dilutes the potency of learning. They might step in at the last minute and rework a key presentation a direct report is responsible for producing. They intervene when an internal customer is dissatisfied. All of this subtly tells people they are not smart enough to figure things out on their own. The next time around the employee might exert even less effort, knowing their manager will step in.

Allowing consequences to have their effect allows natural forces to inform intelligent action. It communicates that the manager believes people are smart enough to figure things out. People become more independent because they feel they own both their actions and the result or consequences of those actions. Investors want their investments to be successful, but they know they can't intervene and alter natural market forces. By providing the possibility to fail, these leaders give others the freedom and the motivation to grow and succeed. Elaben Bhatt captured this well when she said, "There are risks in every action. Every success has the seed of some failure."

Make the Scoreboard Visible

When the scoreboard is visible, people hold themselves accountable. Whether it is in sports, business, or community service, visible measures of success liberate and focus intelligence and energy.

Jubin Dana is a lawyer by day and a professional soccer coach by night. Perhaps it is his training as a lawyer that shapes his coaching system, which boils down to one simple but powerful technique: He keeps stats. He tracks the players' sprinting and distance running times. He measures their number of passes and tracks their success rates in soccer team tackle drills and their shots-on-goal. He tracks and posts all these statistics for all the players to see. The players can easily tell where their skills rank and where they need to improve. Armed with this information, they no longer need a coach yelling at them to run faster or try harder. They tend to push themselves to higher levels of performance.

Multipliers have a core belief that *people are smart and will figure things out.* So it makes sense that they operate as Investors, giving ownership that keeps rolling back to other people. They invest the resources they need to grow a business and the people in it. They engage personally, offering their insight and guidance, but they remember to "give the pen back" when they are done so people remain accountable to deliver on the expected returns.

By playing the role of Investor, Multipliers generate independence. They create organizations that can sustain performance without their direct involvement. When the organization is truly autonomous, they have earned the right to step away. When they leave, they leave a legacy.

THE DIMINISHER'S APPROACH TO EXECUTION

The Diminisher operates from a very different assumption: *People will never be able to figure it out without me.* They believe if they don't dive into the details and follow up, other people won't deliver. These assumptions breed dependency as full ownership is never offered up. They assign piecemeal tasks but jump in believing that other people cannot make it work without them.

Unfortunately, in the end, these assumptions are often proven true as people become disabled and dependent on the Diminisher for answers, for approval, and to integrate the pieces together. When this happens, Diminishers look outward, asking themselves only, *Why are people always letting me down?* When Diminishers eventually leave an organization, things fall apart. Things crumble because the leader has held the operation together with micromanagement and sweat equity.

Consider the case of a private equity investor in Brazil who stifled his entire organization with his micromanagement.

Celso is extraordinarily smart and considered by his colleagues to be a financial genius. He was a superior analyst and a rock star of a stock trader. But his control-freak management style hampered his ability to build great companies. Unfortunately, as the head of a private equity firm, his job was exactly that: to build companies.

In staff meetings, his staff rarely got through their reports on prospective investments or portfolio companies. He would interrupt with his pithy analysis. Sure, he'd make a few great points, but it discouraged other people from thinking. His signature remark was, "I can't believe you haven't figured this out."

Celso tracked performance of their portfolio companies with second-by-second monitoring and arranged to receive all company sales reports on his cell phone. When sales dipped off target, he'd call the CEO at random hours of the night and start screaming. Whatever the situation, Celso was the first to respond. Like Pavlov's dog, there was no delay between stimulus and response. When he found a problem, he'd jump in immediately and try to fix it himself.

Over time, Celso's micromanagement created a sharp division inside the organization. Most of his colleagues would lie low, knowing that he eventually would do things himself. As much of the talent retreated, he compensated by hiring aggressive graduates of elite colleges who didn't have enough experience to expect a different type of leadership. The organization began to look a lot like Celso over time and resembled an alpha-male annual convention. Like many Diminishers, Celso's micromanagement stifled the intelligence inside of an organization filled with really smart people.

Let's look at the ways in which these Diminishers cripple the capability of their people and create dependent organizations.

MAINTAIN OWNERSHIP. The approach of the Micromanager is well captured in a comment made by a staff member of a prominent professor: "I can't make any decisions. I don't have lead in my pencil until Dr. Yang says that I do." Diminishers don't trust others to figure it out for themselves, so they maintain ownership. When they delegate, they dole out piecemeal tasks but not real responsibility. They give people just a piece of the puzzle. It is no wonder that people have a hard time putting the puzzle together without them.

Eva Wiesel is smart and energetic, but most unfortunately for her team, quite a morning person. She was the operations manager in a manufacturing plant and each day she'd come to work with a fresh set of ideas for her management team. She would plan out the day on her commute into work, arrive at the plant, walk through the door, and begin dropping by her people's office to let them know exactly what she wanted them to do that day. Some days it was more of the same, but other days the tasks took them in entirely new directions. Her people noticed the pattern and began a simple coping routine. Every day about 8:00 a.m., they began lining up in the hallway that led from the lobby to their office area. With pads of paper and coffee in hand, they waited for her to burst in and deliver their "marching orders" for the day. It was just easier for everyone to wait to be told what to do.

No doubt, Eva thought she was a great leader who was delegating and communicating clearly to her team. In reality, Eva was a Micromanager who did all the thinking for her team and hoarded the ownership of the work.

JUMP IN AND OUT. Micromanagers hand over work to others, but they take it back the moment problems arise. They get lured in like a fish to the shiny objects on a fisherman's line. Emergent problems and big hurdles are irresistible bait for Diminishers. They see these shiny objects and are attracted. They are fascinated by the intellectual challenge to solve the problem. They are lured by the attention and kudos they get for saving the day. And they are hooked on the feeling of importance as people become dependent on them and their brilliance to deliver results. They are lured in, and the diminishing impact on their people is set.

The problem is that they don't just get lured in and stay there. They come in and out. An issue gets onto the radar screen of senior management, and suddenly they are all over it. They spring in and then when the fun is over, they spring back out. They are the bungee boss.

Garth Yamamoto is the chief marketing officer for a consumer products company. Garth has two modes: One is "all over it" and the other is "completely absent." When his team is working on an issue with CEO visibility, he jumps in, takes over, and delivers the work straight to his boss, a highly mercurial leader. When the CEO isn't involved, Garth is nowhere to be seen. His people struggle to get his attention on the less visible but equally critical projects that form the backbone of the business.

When these leaders bungee in and out of their own organization, they create dependency and disengagement. When they strike at random, they produce disruptive chaos.

TAKE IT BACK. I was twenty-five years old and six months into my first management job. It was 7:30 p.m., as I sat at my desk at 500 Oracle Parkway, Oracle's main office tower. The halls were dark and all of my staff had gone home for the night. Everyone was home but me. I was still busy trying to close out my "to dos" for the day, many of which had emerged during the course of the workday as one little crisis after another landed on my desk. I came up from my absorption in my work and thought, *Why am I still doing so much of the work? I've delegated. Why does it all come back to me?* People were bringing me their problems, and I would take them back.

At this realization, I became irritated at my team for dumping the problems on me and for not doing their jobs. Then, alone in a dark office, I had the epiphany: I wasn't doing *my* job. As a manager, my job was no longer about me. It was my responsibility to manage the work, not do the work. I had been solving problems like some overzealous superhero, when I was really supposed to help other people solve problems. My job was to flow the work to my team and keep it there. It is an embarrassingly simple idea, but for me as a newly promoted manager, it was a startling realization.

As I coach executives, I am frequently surprised at how many senior leaders and even executives haven't discovered this simple lesson. When managers take it back, not only do they end up doing all the work but they rob others of the opportunity to use and extend their own intelligence. They stunt the growth of intelligence around them. They begin to slide down the slippery slope of the Accidental Diminisher.

Whether accidental or not, Diminishers are costly to organizations.

They might be superstars themselves, but they quickly become the gating factor that limits the growth of their organizations. The cost of the Micromanager is that organizations cannot grow beyond them and struggle to leverage the other intellect inside the organization.

LEVERAGING YOUR INVESTMENT

Multipliers don't act as Investors because it makes people feel good. They invest because they value the return on their investment. They believe that people perform at their best when they have a natural accountability. So they define ownership, invest resources, and hold people accountable.

The following chart illustrates why Micromanagers leave capability on the table while Investors stretch the capability of their resources:

Micromanagers		Investors	
What They Do	*What They Get*	*What They Do*	*What They Get*
Manage every detail of the work to ensure it is completed the way they would do it	People who wait to be told what to do People who hold back because they expect to be interrupted and told what to do instead Free riders who wait for the boss to swoop in and save them People who try to "work" their bosses and make sophisticated excuses	Give other people the ownership for results and invest in their success	People who take initiative and anticipate challenges People who are fully focused on achieving results People who can get ahead of the boss in solving problems People who respond to the natural forces around them

Micromanagers don't use the full complement of talent, intelligence, and resourcefulness that is available to them. This capacity sits idle in their organizations. To counteract this, they continue to ask the organization for more resources, wondering why people aren't more productive and are always letting them down.

In contrast to this, Investors not only engage people through clearly delegating responsibilities to them, they extend assignments that stretch the thinking and capability of the individuals and the team. They grow the assets in their portfolio. As a result, they get full leverage out of their current resources and they stretch and increase the capacity of the organization to take on the next responsibility.

The Serial Multiplier

After seven hours of conversation in a studio apartment next to one of Mumbai's slums, Narayana Murthy and six of his friends agreed to a vision for a software firm in Bangalore that they hoped would do two things. First, persuade their wives to each contribute $250 as seed money. Second, garner respect around the world. They accomplished both.

Their investment of intellectual energy and financial capital turned out to be very sound, as Mr. Murthy led Infosys Technologies from its tiny beginnings to become the first Indian company to be listed on the NASDAQ, with a valuation of $10 billion. Mr. Murthy helped his team reach beyond their dreams, encouraged India's entrepreneurs to believe in themselves, and gave a face to the new India.

He became a revered name inside and outside the company and could have easily stayed at the top and enjoyed the fame and power of his exalted position.

Instead, on his sixtieth birthday, Mr. Murthy stepped aside as CEO. No crisis triggered the move and there was no power play to topple him. The move was the extension of a deliberate plan. He had spent years investing in the other cofounders so they could operate independently of him. Consistent with his plan, he handed the role of CEO over to one of the other cofounders, Nandan Nilekani. Mr. Murthy stayed on as nonexecutive chairman and chief mentor of the company.

Asked at the World Economic Forum in Davos, Switzerland, why he chose that role for himself, he said his primary role as a leader was to ensure successive generations of leaders. When asked what drives him to invest in this way, he said without hesitation, "The reward for winning a pinball game is to get a chance to play the next one." In other words, he doesn't crave the spotlight of being a CEO as much as he hungers to freely invest again elsewhere. While some CEOs are addicted to praise, Mr. Murthy is addicted to growing other people. A Multiplier to his core, Mr. Murthy recognized that his greatest value was not in his intelligence, but in how he invested his intelligence in others. And now in his second career, he has again been investing in the growth of others, just with a much broader sphere of influence.

Free from the operational management responsibilities at Infosys, he has gone on to invest in governments and institutions around the world, including Thailand and the United Nations, and educational entities like Cornell University, the Wharton School of Business, and Singapore Management University. He has the ear of the prime minister of India and is making a case to him to invest in the next generation. In his words, "We have to put young people in charge of these massive educational initiatives." And his investor approach to management has established a pattern at Infosys.

When leaders like Mr. Murthy invest in the development of other leaders, they earn the right to step away without jeopardizing the performance of the organization. The Investor not only reaps these rewards but is now available to repeat the investment cycle elsewhere.

Much like a serial entrepreneur who builds one successful company after another, these leaders can become Serial Multipliers. Of course, doing so requires the leader to break free of the addiction to praise that entraps many senior leaders and instead become addicted to growth—growth of the business and growth of the people around them. Serial Multipliers grow intelligence. This intelligence isn't ephemeral, fleeing when the Multiplier is no longer by their side. It is real, and it is sustainable, which is what allows the Multiplier to replicate the effect again and again.

BECOMING AN INVESTOR

But to become a Serial Multiplier (or serial entrepreneur), you have to have a starting point and a first success to begin the positively addictive cycle. Here are four strategies for becoming an Investor.

The Starting Block

1. LET THEM KNOW WHO IS BOSS. When you delegate, you probably let people know what you are expecting of them. But take this to the next level and let people know that they (not you) are in charge and accountable. Tell them how you will stay engaged and support them, but that they remain in charge. Give them a number to make it concrete. For example, tell them they have 51 percent of the vote and that you have only 49 percent. Or be bold and make it a 75/25 split.

Give them charge of something that requires them to stretch beyond their current capabilities. Start with ownership for the current scope of their role, and then take it up one level. Look for ways to up-level their responsibility and give them a job that they aren't fully qualified for.

2. LET NATURE TAKE ITS COURSE. Nature is the most powerful teacher. We can easily forget this when consequences are artificially imposed on us. But we remember and learn deeply when we experience the natural consequences of our actions.

Several years ago, our family took a vacation to Maui, Hawaii.

We parked ourselves on the beach at the very end of Ka'anapali, at the base of Black Rock point. It is a beautiful beach, but because it is there that the ocean confronts the huge rock jutting out of the beach, the surf can be rough. My three-year-old son Christian was fascinated by the ocean and kept straying out of the baby waves and into the dangerous surf. The scene is familiar to every parent. He would venture out too far, then I would go fetch him back, get down at eye level, and tell him about the power of the ocean and why it was too dangerous for him to be out this far. He would resume playing, forget my teaching, and venture out again. We repeated this futile cycle several times.

I decided it was time for him to learn the lesson from Mother Nature instead of from Mom. I watched for a mid-size wave to come toward shore. I selected one that would give him a good topple but wouldn't sweep him off to Japan. Instead of pulling him back in as the wave approached, I let him venture out. And rather than grabbing his arm and lifting him out of the water, I simply stood by his side. Several parents nearby looked alarmed as they saw the wave coming. One tried to get my attention by giving me that "bad mother" look. I assured him I was on duty but as more of a teacher than a lifeguard. The wave came in and instantly dragged Christian under the surf and tossed him around several times. After he'd had a good tumble, I pulled my three-year-old back up to safety. Once he caught his breath and spit out the sand, we had a talk about the power of the ocean. This time he seemed to understand, and now stayed closer to shore. He continues to love the ocean and to body surf, but displays a respect for the power of nature.

Nature teaches best. When we let nature take its course and allow people to experience the natural consequences of their actions, they learn most rapidly and most profoundly. When we protect people from experiencing the natural ramifications of their actions, we stunt their learning. Real intelligence gets developed through experimentation and by trial and error.

Letting nature teach is hard, because our managerial performance instincts kick in. We want to ensure that our team delivers successfully. The good news is that you don't need to let a major project fail. Find the "smaller waves" that will provide natural teaching moments, without catastrophic outcomes. To let nature teach, try these steps:

1. *Let it happen.* Don't jump in and fix an assignment so it doesn't fail. Don't take over a meeting because someone isn't handling it well. Let the person experience a degree of failure.

2. *Talk about it.* Be available to help someone learn from the failure. Be standing by after a failed meeting or lost sales deal to help them get up, brush off the sand, and talk about what happened. Ask great questions and avoid the ever-diminishing, "I told you so."

3. *Focus on next time.* Help them find a way to be successful next time. Give them a way out and a path forward. If they've just botched an important sales call, ask them how they'll handle a similar situation with another customer in their pipeline.

Not only are there natural consequences to our mistakes, there are natural consequences to good decisions. Allow people to experience the full force of their successes. Step out of the way, give them credit, and let them reap the full benefits of their victories.

3. ASK FOR THE F-I-X. Many people are promoted into management positions because they are natural problem solvers. So when someone brings you a problem, it is only natural for you to want to fix it. And chances are, people will expect you to because you so often do. In that split second before you respond, recall Kerry Patterson marching into the office of his intern and demanding she do more than just point out awkward sentences. Ask for people to complete the thought process and provide a fix. Use simple questions such as:

- What solution(s) do you see to this problem?

- How would you propose we solve this?

- What would you like to do to fix this?

Most important, don't assume responsibility for fixing the problem. Put the problem back on their desk and encourage them to stretch further. When someone brings you an A-W-K, ask for an F-I-X.

4. HAND BACK THE PEN. When someone is stuck and asks you for your opinion, it can be hard not to take over. For some, the tendency to take over is so great that they sit on their hands afraid to speak out lest it turn into a hostile takeover. When you see your team members are struggling, offer help, but have an exit plan. These conversations can happen anywhere—in a conference room, sitting in your office one-on-one, or during a spontaneous meeting in the hallway. Regardless of the venue, visualize the point in the conversation when you can symbolically give the pen back. Imagine yourself at the whiteboard, adding a few ideas to the collective thinking on the board. You finish your thought and then hand the pen back. This gesture lets your colleagues know they are still in the lead and are accountable to finish the job.

Here are some statements that signal that you are handing back the pen:

- I'm happy to help think this through, but I'm still looking to you to lead this going forward.

- You are still in the lead on this.

- I'm here to back you up. What do you need from me as you lead this?

Each of the above is a simple entry point. But done repetitively these actions can instigate the Multiplier effect inside your organization.

THE MULTIPLIER EFFECT

When Multipliers invest resources and confidence in other people and give them the ownership of their success, they uncover the vast intelligence and capability that lies within. Muhammad Yunus, 2006 Nobel laureate and father of the microcredit movement said, "Each person has tremendous potential. She or he alone can influence the lives of others within the communities, nations, within and beyond her or his own time."

Multipliers invest in others in a way that builds independence to allow others to apply their full intelligence to the work at hand, and also to expand their scope and influence. The independence they create in others also allows the Investor to reinvest over and over, becoming a Serial Multiplier. The math is simple but powerful. The immediate Multiplier effect is that Multipliers get, on average, twice the capability from someone they lead. When extrapolated across an average organization size of approximately fifty people, that's the equivalent of adding an additional fifty people. Repeated over potentially ten different leadership roles over the course of a career, that is an additional 500 people.

Multipliers continually double the size of their workforce for free. This 2X return in perpetuity for leading like a Multiplier makes a compelling business case, even to the most discerning investors on Sand Hill Road.

THE MULTIPLIER FORMULA

THE MICROMANAGER VERSUS THE INVESTOR

MICROMANAGERS manage every detail in a way that creates dependence on the leader and their presence for the organization to perform.

INVESTORS give other people the investment and ownership they need to produce results independent of the leader.

The Three Practices of the Investor

1. *Define Ownership*
   - Name the lead
   - Give ownership for the end goal
   - Stretch the role

2. *Invest Resources*
   - Teach and coach
   - Provide backup

3. *Hold People Accountable*
   - Give it back
   - Expect complete work
   - Respect natural consequences
   - Make the scoreboard visible

Becoming an Investor

1. Let them know who is boss
2. Let nature take its course
3. Ask for the F-I-X
4. Hand back the pen

Unexpected Findings

1. Multipliers do get involved in the operational details, but they keep the ownership with other people.

2. Multipliers are rated 42% higher at delivering world-class results than their Diminisher counterparts.[3]

CHAPTER 7

BECOMING A MULTIPLIER

When I let go of what I am,
I become what I might be.

LAO TZU

Bill Campbell, former CEO of Intuit, began his career over thirty years ago as a collegiate football coach at an Ivy League university. As a coach he was smart, aggressive, and hard-hitting. When he was recruited into the consumer technology business, he operated in much the same way. As a young marketing manager at Kodak, he would take over and rewrite the sales leaders' business plans if he saw them failing. While working under detail-oriented John Scully at Apple Computer, Bill became the ultimate Micromanager. He burrowed into every detail in the business and directed every decision and action. He said, "I drove everyone nuts. I was a real Diminisher. Believe me, I made every decision and I pushed everyone around. I was really bad."

Confessions of a Diminisher

Bill recalls one of his worst moments. During an important staff meeting, one member of his management team asked a simple question. Bill, annoyed at the uninformed manager, turned to him and sharply replied (replete with colorful language), "That's the dumbest question I have ever heard." The room went silent. Bill continued the meeting, uninterrupted by any other annoying questions. Over the next few weeks, he noticed that most everyone stopped asking him questions. He had dismantled the group's curiosity.

While at Claris as CEO, his hard-hitting leadership continued. A close colleague came to him and confided, "Hey Bill, we all came here because we liked working for you at the last company. But you are back to your old ways. You are pushing everyone around and making all the decisions." Bill knew she was right.

And this wasn't the only near-mutiny. Two months into starting another company, one member of his management team approached him and said, "I am here representing the whole group. If you don't let us do our jobs, we are going to regret coming here. We don't want to leave, but we need to be able to do our jobs." Bill knew he was calling in plays at fourth down and one yard to go. He knew it was hurting his company and jeopardizing his team of exceptionally smart players. And he wasn't willing to lose them.

Becoming a Multiplier

The counsel from two bold colleagues was just the dose of self-awareness that Bill needed. He could see his need for a course correction, and he made it. He started by listening more and telling less. He began to develop a deep appreciation for what his colleagues knew. And as he recognized the diminishing effect he had on his management team, he began to detect other Diminishers in his organization. He began to counsel them. He recalled one person in particular who chronically needed to prove he was the smartest guy in the room. Bill sat him down and explained, "I don't care how brilliant you are yourself. If you keep this up, you are going to bring the organization to its knees. You are terrific, but you can't work here like this."

Bill became a better leader over time. It was a steady transition that happened naturally out of his desire to preserve his team and to realize the value of the incredible talent that he had attracted. By the time Bill became CEO at Intuit and led the company past the $1 billion revenue mark in 2000, he had uncovered the Multiplier inside of him.

A Multiplier of Multipliers

Since retiring from his role as CEO, Bill has remained on the Intuit board, but spends his time coaching early-stage start-up companies. He plays the role of mentor—a leader who has been there before, made the mistakes, and learned from those mistakes. He works closely with venture capital partners, and their respective roles are clear: the VCs invest, and Bill grows the talent. He develops the CEO and the key leaders so the company can grow to its market potential.

What does Bill do to cultivate the CEOs? To a great extent, he builds Multipliers. He teaches what he learned himself and claims, "If it can be learned, it can be taught." He helps these highly intelligent (and often young) CEOs learn how to leverage the intelligence inside their own organization. And the CEOs he has coached have progressed to build some of technology's most prominent companies—Amazon.com, Netscape, PayPal, Google, and many more.

Recently Bill helped one CEO transform his executive staff meetings from bland functional report-out sessions to rigorous debates on the jugular business issues. Before, the meetings followed a predictable format: Each person around the table would give their report, informing their colleagues of progress being made and issues within their function. Bill sat in on many of these staff meetings and saw the underutilization of the enormous brainpower in the room. He counseled, "You are not getting anything out of these staff meetings. You need to engage your people on your biggest issues." Bill asked the CEO to prepare five topics that were crucial to the company. The CEO then e-mailed the list to the team in advance and asked each person to think through the issue and come prepared with data and opinions.

The CEO opened the next meeting by asking his management team to take off their functional hat and put their company hat on. He then launched into the first issue: Should we be in the services space or should we give this business to our partners? One executive cited the reasons they should stay in the space. Another argued the contrary. Each member of the team chimed in with his and her perspectives. The CEO listened carefully, made the decision, and then outlined the implications and actions. One team member stepped up and said, "I've got it. I'll take it from here." The CEO then moved onto the next topic, and the next debate ensued.

Bill reflects on his work coaching and advising some of Silicon Valley's rock-star CEOs. He says, "I can help them see it differently. I kick them out of their comfort zones and I ask them the hard questions."

Bill began his career as a Diminisher telling people what to do and calling all the plays. Now he plays the role of the Multiplier where he asks the hard questions that make others think. But his leadership journey didn't end there. Bill Campbell is not just a Multiplier, he has become a multiplier of Multipliers, building other powerful leaders who can extract and multiply intelligence and capability around them.

Bill's journey from Diminisher to multiplier of Multipliers is similar to those of other leaders we studied and raises a number of questions. Can someone with Diminisher roots actually become a Multiplier? Can the transition be authentic? Does this journey happen passively over time through the wisdom that comes of maturity? Or can it be accelerated through active effort? In this chapter, we'll address these questions and explore the journey of becoming a Multiplier. We'll offer examples of leaders making the transition and provide you with a framework and a set of tools to help you choose to lead more like a Multiplier.

FROM RESONANCE TO RESOLVE

As various people have heard these ideas and read this book, I have observed a nearly universal three-step reaction:

1. *Resonance.* People tell us that the distinction between Diminishers and Multipliers vividly reflects their reality and that they have experienced these dynamics in action. They usually remark, "Yes, I have worked for this guy!"

2. *Realization of the Accidental Diminisher.* Virtually all readers have confessed that they see some degree of a Diminisher within themselves. For some, there are only trace amounts. For others, it is a chronic pattern of behavior. They realize that their well-meaning management practices are, in all probability, having a diminishing effect on the people they work with.

3. *Resolve to be a Multiplier.* After identifying their own Diminisher tendencies, they build conviction to become more of a Multiplier. They have a genuine desire, but are often overwhelmed by the standard of the Multiplier and the apparent magnitude of the task of becoming one.

Having spent over eighteen years in management roles in corporations myself, I recognize why learning to lead like a Multiplier can feel overwhelming. For a start, many national and organizational cultures lean to the Diminisher side; Multiplier leadership isn't often the norm. The path of least resistance is frequently the path of the Diminisher. And while I appreciate the challenge, I also have worked with leaders who have grown, become Multipliers, and realized the benefits of this approach. It is not hard to be a Multiplier, but it is definitely easier to be a Diminisher.

Twin Obstacles

There are two obstacles many people encounter as they consider the Multiplier approach to leadership. Let's address each of them in turn.

1. STUCK UNDERNEATH A DIMINISHER. I hear the following said often by aspiring Multipliers: "I want to lead this way, but my boss doesn't, so I can't." Herein lies the notorious boss factor.

I heard this first from an executive vice president in a large corporation. Jim had grown up in a home where intelligence was prized and not having the answer was punished. Fortunately, Jim was smart, performed well in school, and went on to gain an elite university education and build a successful career. The foundation of his career was his superior knowledge of the market and the business he ran. In his current role, this dynamic was exacerbated because he worked for a president who was brilliant but who was also a bona fide Diminisher. Jim had a significant problem because his own need to know it all was shutting down the intelligence of the people around him. He got feedback, recognized the problem, and wanted to become a better leader. In contemplating the new mindsets and practices of a Multiplier, he became hopeful, even enthusiastic. He experimented with some of the practices and received resoundingly positive feedback from his colleagues and employees. However, his hope turned to discouragement as he began wondering how his boss would react. He said, "This isn't going to work. You know my boss. He doesn't lead this way, so why should I?"

He had a good point. I did know his boss, and I knew Jim wouldn't receive much support from him. But I also knew that he wouldn't encounter active resistance, either. And I knew the organization would perform better if he managed like a Multiplier, and the results would speak for themselves. I asked him, "Jim, has it ever occurred to you that you could be a better leader than your boss?" By the reaction on his face, I could tell it hadn't. I asked again, "What would happen if you gave yourself permission to be better than your boss?"

He was struck, and perhaps even liberated, by this idea that he didn't have to imitate and be limited by the leadership of his superiors. I watched as he assumed a new approach to leadership—one in which he asked more than he told and shined the spotlight on the knowledge of others rather than on himself. I watched as he outgrew his boss and went on to become CEO of two companies.

There is a hidden assumption in many organizations that people are not expected, or even allowed, to out-lead their bosses. The layers of the org chart appear to form a glass ceiling that caps leadership effectiveness. Is it possible that a Multiplier can thrive in a Diminisher environment? Can you be a Multiplier while working for a Diminisher boss? Given the extraordinary results that Multipliers achieve through others, I believe you can. Give yourself permission to be better than your boss. And then watch the organization take notice.

2. OVERLOADED AND OVERWHELMED. A second, related obstacle aspiring Multipliers often face is feeling overwhelmed. They are typically already functioning on overload and cannot find the time needed to fund their development. This time crunch is particularly acute for any leader who has been operating as a Diminisher, because after all, it takes a lot of time to be a tyrannical, micromanaging know-it-all! And it sucks much-needed time and energy to work for one. Diminishers not only drain others, they can exhaust themselves trying to stay on top.

Yes, becoming a Multiplier requires an investment. It takes initial effort to understand one's current impact on others and to formulate new approaches. But becoming a Multiplier doesn't necessitate extra work. It doesn't have to be hard. You can take the lazy way. In fact, the lazy way works best.

Take the Lazy Way

Professionally speaking, I was raised among overachieving, type-A, driver-drivers. So it often surprises my clients when I suggest they take the lazy way.

Let me explain. I've noticed that the more important something is, the more likely a lazy man's approach will work best. When something is based on sound design, it doesn't need to be forced. It just needs the right amount of effort applied in exactly the right place or in the right way. Suppose you are repairing an appliance at home, and you need to open a casing by loosening a six-sided hex screw. You grab a pair of pliers from the drawer, and with the pliers gripping two sides of the nut, you begin twisting. You pull, you turn, but you can't get a good grip. You try the pliers on a different two sides, hoping it will be easier. You break a sweat trying to loosen this nut, but you can't get it to budge. Your tool-savvy roommate sees your futile effort, and hands you a hex nut ratchet. This specially designed tool encases the nut and provides preset torque and leverage. You place this tool around the nut, and with virtually no effort, the nut turns and loosens.

You can learn to lead like a Multiplier by following this same principle. You can do it the hard way by tackling everything at once. You can attempt to apply all five disciplines, all the time and all the way. Chances are you will exert great effort but show little progress and will eventually give up. Or you can take the lazy way, and with the right approach and tools, make sustainable progress without overwhelming yourself or others.

Below are three lazy-way strategies or accelerators that can propel you on your journey to become a Multiplier. Any one of these, or all three together, will accelerate your development and enable you to attain maximum results with just the right amount of effort.

Accelerator	How It Works
1. Work the Extremes.	Assess your leadership practices and then focus your development on the two extremes: 1) bring up your lowest low and 2) take your highest high to the next level.
2. Start with the Assumptions.	Adopt the assumptions of a Multiplier and allow the behavior and practices to naturally follow.
3. Take the 30-Day Multiplier Challenge.	Pick one practice within one discipline, and work it for 30 days.

With the right approach, leading like a Multiplier is within reach. Some people will stumble into it over time, while others will never learn it and will possibly remain ignorant of their diminishing effect on those around them. But the assumptions and the five disciplines of the Multiplier can be learned, and this learning can be accelerated.

Let's consider a few examples of those who have taken their first steps and are just beginning to experience the payback. I'll share their stories and then outline the accelerators and tools that worked for them.

THE ACCELERATORS

Accelerator #1: Work the Extremes

In 2002, Jack Zenger and Joe Folkman published a set of fascinating research findings in their book *The Extraordinary Leader*.[1] They studied 360 degree assessment data for 8,000 leaders, looking for what differentiated the extraordinary leaders from the average leaders. They found that leaders who were perceived as having no distinguishing strengths were rated at the thirty-fourth percentile of effectiveness of all leaders in the study. However, when a leader was perceived as having just one distinguishing strength, his or her effectiveness shot to the sixty-fourth percentile. Having one towering strength almost doubled the effectiveness of the leader, provided the leader had no area of sharp weakness. Leaders with two, three, and four strengths jump to the seventy-second, eighty-first, and eighty-ninth percentile respectively. The Zenger-Folkman study demonstrates that leaders do not need to be good at everything. They need to have mastery of a small number of skills and be free of show-stopper weaknesses.

What does this imply for someone aspiring to lead like a Multiplier? It means that you do not need to excel at each of the Multiplier disciplines and master every practice. As we studied Multipliers, we noticed that each individual Multiplier wasn't necessarily, or even typically, strong in all five disciplines. The majority of Multipliers were strong in just three. There were many who were strong in four or even all five, but having strength in three of the disciplines appears to be a threshold for Multiplier status. We also noticed that these Multipliers were rarely in the Diminisher range in any of the five disciplines. A leader does not have to be exceptional in all five disciplines to be considered a Multiplier. A leader needs two or three strong disciplines and the other disciplines can be just good enough.

Spencer Kaplan[2] is a director of sales operations for a global consumer products company. In this role, Spencer manages the operational infrastructure that enables the sales teams and works across several sales channels and sales leaders. The organization made an investment in Spencer to ready him for a larger, more complex role supporting the entire global business.

Spencer launched a 360 degree feedback process and met with his coach to review the data. After reviewing the results of the 360 degree feedback, he was inundated with the plethora of data and was unsure of which skills he should develop. But as he filtered the data, searching for the extremes (the highest highs and the show-stopper lows), two critical development targets emerged.

First, his chief strength was readily apparent. The organization viewed him as a trusted advisor. His colleagues trusted his judgment and his objective analysis and knew that he operated entirely without ego. He was known for his ability to gather players from across the organization and use these people to develop collaborative solutions. Second, his vulnerability was also obvious. While the organization viewed him as a rock star, his peers and various bosses were concerned that the capability gap between him and his team was too large. While he was advising the rest of the organization, he hadn't been sufficiently investing in his own team. The feedback from the stakeholders was clear: They could not expand his role unless his team members were growing their abilities as fast as he was.

Spencer and his coach built a two-pronged development plan. The first priority was to shore up his vulnerability by investing in his immediate team. He identified several practices of the Investor to work on: giving real ownership to his team, expanding their roles, and expecting complete work. After giving his managers greater ownership, he would step back and coach, allowing natural consequences to teach and develop them.

With this work well under way, Spencer began topping off his strength as a trusted advisor. His aim was to go beyond just developing collaborative solutions. He wanted to be able to lead the most rigorous of debates. Spencer worked in a data-savvy organization, so the role of the Debate Maker was a natural extension of his strength as a trusted advisor. He began to tackle the tough business issues that were going unresolved. He focused his development on these practices: gathering the critical players, framing the issues, and leading rigorous, data-rich debates.

With these two development goals clear, Spencer disregarded most of the other feedback. He continued to naturally practice and refine many of the other practices of the Multiplier, but his purposeful development was clear: focus on the extremes by topping off his biggest strength and neutralizing a weakness that would prevent the growth of his team, himself, and perhaps even the company.

Instead of trying to develop strength in all five disciplines, an aspiring Multiplier should set an extreme development plan. Begin by assessing your leadership practices and then work the two extremes: 1) neutralize a weakness and 2) top off a strength.

Based on the research in this book, we've developed a multirater assessment tool that you can find at www.multipliersbook.com. Taking this 360-degree assessment will get you started in identifying your relative strengths along the Diminisher–Multiplier continuum. When reviewing your report, look for your extremes. Which discipline is your strongest? Are any disciplines dangerously within Diminisher territory? With this information, pursue these two strategies:

1. *Neutralize a weakness.* A common misconception in executive coaching is that coaching or development can—or even should—turn your weaknesses into strengths. Clients have often told me, "I'm terrible at this and I need to become really great at it." I suggest to them that while this may be possible, it is unlikely that they will turn their biggest weaknesses into their biggest strengths. The truth is that you do not need to be fabulous at everything. You just can't be bad. You simply need to neutralize the weakness and move it into the middle, acceptable zone. Having realistic goals frees up capacity to do the most important development work: turning your modest strengths into towering strengths.

2. *Top off a strength.* As Zenger and Folkman and many others have found, leaders with a small number of strengths are viewed more highly than leaders who have a broad base of capabilities. Of the five disciplines, identify your strongest area and then build a deep and broad repertoire of practices that allows you to excel at this discipline. Become a world-class Challenger or a resounding Talent Magnet. Invest your energy wisely and progress from good to great by topping off one of your strengths.

The following chart illustrates these two development strategies:

WORKING THE EXTREMES—DEVELOPMENT STRATEGY

	Multiplier	Talent Magnet	Liberator	Challenger	Debate Maker	Investor
Towering Strength		⬆ 2				
Competency			●	●		●
Vulnerablity					⬆ 1	
Diminisher		Empire Builder	Tyrant	Know-It-All	Decision Maker	Micro manager

(Left vertical axis label: Diminisher to Multiplier Performance Continuum)

Working the extremes by paying attention to your highs and lows while ignoring the middle offers an efficient and sustainable pathway to leadership development. The strategies above can become more pinpointed through a rigorous multirater assessment. In addition to working the extremes, you can also accelerate your development by adopting the assumptions of a Multiplier.

Accelerator #2: Start with the Assumptions

To score a strike in ten-pin bowling, you need to hit the head pin. Hitting the head pin directly will knock down most of the pins behind it; hitting it in just the right place, on the left or right side, allows the bowler to knock down all the pins in a single strike. The assumptions of a Multiplier are the head pin to becoming one. Because behavior follows assumptions, you can knock out a whole set of behaviors by adopting the right belief. Consider the following scenario and how you might approach it with either a Diminisher or Multiplier assumption.

You are about to start your weekly one-on-one with your marketing manager Jyanthi Gupta. Another executive has asked that you appoint someone from your division as a representative on a cross-divisional task force that will assess the company's competitive position and recommend changes to the current marketing programs. You decide to put Jyanthi on the task force and plan to use this one-on-one meeting to tee up this assignment.

FROM A DIMINISHER ASSUMPTION: How would you approach this meeting if you assume, *people will never figure this out without me?* How would you define Jyanthi's role? What role would you take? How would you explain the assignment? How would you monitor progress?

With this assumption, you would probably use Jyanthi as your representative—your eyes and ears into this project. She would attend the meetings, gather information, and then report back so you can weigh in on the issues. You would probably explain the assignment by telling her that she is representing you and how important it is that she not give anyone the wrong impression about what is happening in your division.

What is the result of this approach? Jyanthi spends a lot of time attending meetings, but contributes very little to the task force. She is careful to not overstep her role, so she passes up opportunities to speak out and steers clear of any controversial issues where she might be called on to influence a decision. You provide input at a couple junctions, but most of the important decisions happened live, during the meetings. At the conclusion of the task force, you find that several decisions were made that are not in the best interest of your division. And you hear through the grapevine that the task force leader commented about the lack of engagement from your division.

FROM A MULTIPLIER ASSUMPTION: How would you approach this differently if you believed, *people are smart and can figure it out?*

You would be clear that you chose Jyanthi for her understanding of the market and her ability to assimilate the vast amounts of market data that the task force is assembling. You would let her know that she was representing the entire division and that she was fully responsible for implementing the task force's outcomes. You might recommend she come to meetings armed with data so she can weigh in on the issues and think on her feet during the debates. You would let her know that this task force is her project, but that you are available as a sounding board if she wants to jointly think through the issues.

What are the results of this approach? Jyanthi engages fully in the task force, gains new understanding of the competitive landscape and advocates for marketing programs that will have immediate benefit for your division. She impresses the task force leader who thinks, "This group has great talent."

The assumptions we hold shape our views, our practices, and in the end have a powerful effect on the outcomes, often forming a self-fulfilling prophecy.

One aspiring Multiplier told us that the moment he started shifting his assumptions, he could see new opportunities everywhere. Instead of feeling overwhelmed that he was a bottleneck and frustrated that he had to redo other people's work, he started asking, "How can I improve the situation without putting myself at the center?"

If you want to apply Multiplier skills and behaviors naturally and instinctively, try on the Multiplier assumptions and see how they guide your actions. The chart below summarizes some of the key assumptions of Diminishers and Multipliers that provide this starting point:

Discipline	Diminisher Assumption	Multiplier Assumption
Talent Magnet	*People need to report to me in order to get them to do anything.*	*If I can find someone's genius, I can put them to work.*
Liberator	*Pressure increases performance.*	*People's best thinking must be given, not taken.*
Challenger	*I need to have all the answers.*	*People get smarter by being challenged.*
Debate Maker	*There are only a few people worth listening to.*	*With enough minds, we can figure it out.*
Investor	*People will never be able to figure it out without me.*	*People are smart and will figure things out.*

Accelerator #3: Take a 30-Day Multiplier Challenge

The most effective and enduring learning involves small, successive experimentation with new approaches. When these small experiments produce successful outcomes, the resulting energy fuels the next, slightly bigger experiment. Over time, these experiments form new patterns of behavior that establish a new baseline. One technique to catalyze this cycle of experimentation is to take a 30-Day Multiplier Challenge and focus your efforts on a single discipline for thirty days. Why thirty days? Research shows that it takes approximately thirty days of concentrated effort to form a new habit. Like any good researcher, you should record your experiences in a journal, learning from what works and what doesn't.

Here's a glimpse into what happened when five different leaders, and in some cases their management team, took the 30-Day Challenge. We've highlighted one for each of the five disciplines (and we've changed several names).

LABELING TALENT Jack Bossidy[3] was the team leader in a manufacturing plant. He could see some members of his team dominated meetings while others withdrew. Curiously, the one person who spoke most in the meetings was the one person who felt most underutilized and undervalued.

Jack decided to take a 30-Day Challenge and began by genius watching. He took note of the native genius of each member of his team. In his next staff meeting, he spoke of each person, why they were needed on the team, and the unique capabilities they brought. He went beyond labeling each person's genius one-on-one and labeled it in front of the whole group. The team then reviewed the work that needed to get done over the next quarter and determined assignments. Although not explicitly asked of them, the team naturally ensured each person had an assignment that demanded one or more of his or her unique capabilities.

What do you suppose happened to the undervalued but overly dominating team member? He actually talked less, listened more, and began to draw out the capabilities of the others. Under the leadership of an aspiring Multiplier, he went from dominating to multiplying. He told Jack, "It feels like we are really working as a team now."

LIBERATING LOKESH Christine faced a common management challenge: how to get the most out of a smart but timid colleague. Lokesh always showed deference to other people's ideas. Instead of offering his own opinion, he would just go with what other people recommended. It gave the impression that he didn't have any ideas. Christine found that it was easy to dominate meetings with Lokesh. Without meaning to, she would end up overexpressing her views and speaking 80 percent of the time. The more she tried to rescue him, the worse things seemed to be. The more she "mentored" Lokesh, the less he seemed to contribute.

Christine took the 30-Day Challenge and focused on being a Liberator to Lokesh by making more space for him. She began by asking, "How is Lokesh smart?" The question snapped her out of her more judgmental Diminisher assumptions and put her on a safari. As his abilities came into focus for her (his years of experience and his ability to break complex activities into actionable plans), she found it easier to ask him questions and to give him space to answer them.

Christine noticed an immediate change. Lokesh started to offer opinions. He spoke 50 percent or more in their interactions. He volunteered for the majority of the action items. He stepped into the role of a creator. And within days, one of the clients had commented to Christine about the difference. Christine summarized her learning by saying, "The silence creates the space. The space creates results. The results are valuable. And I have already seen a payoff!"

CHALLENGING STUDENTS Meredith Byrne[4] was in her second year of teaching high school. The class was a specialized topic, which meant four grade levels were in the same class. She was overwhelmed with the enormous range of abilities in her class (one student was taking exams two years ahead of schedule while another was two years behind) and there was no foreseeable way to reduce her class size.

Meredith took the 30-Day Challenge. As she put on her Multiplier glasses, she suddenly saw how underutilized many of her students were. She selected her top all-around student, Bryan, and asked him to assume the role of student leader for the class. She confessed that the role was new and did not yet have clear goals. She seeded some ideas for goals and extended a concrete challenge to him: Define and fulfill this role in a way that next semester the class would continue the tradition.

Bryan went from being a solid student to being an active leader in the class. He selected several other students to work with him, and together they organized academic competitions between their class and other classes in the district—all on their own time. When Meredith asked Bryan how fully he was being engaged, he said that he probably went from 60 to 110 percent. That's an almost two times increase from the person who was already a high performing student. And he increased the engagement of the rest of the class in the process.

DEBATE IN DODGEVILLE Roughly every six months, the inventory management division at Lands End, based in Dodgeville, Wisconsin, would get an urgent request from the executive management team for a new approach to forecasting. When this request comes in, the senior inventory managers typically lock themselves in a room and find a Band-Aid tool that satisfies the immediate request. Inevitably, the Band-Aid comes loose and those people uninvolved and underutilized in the decision-making process were then overworked trying to force the plan to work.

But this time it was different. The entire inventory management team had just signed up for the 30-Day Challenge and selected the Debate Maker discipline for their work. This time, when the urgent request came from senior management, the group prepared for a thorough debate to find a sustainable solution. They brought in senior planners and the IT group (who usually had to scramble after the fact), who could give practical input to the feasibility of any suggested solution. They framed the issues and set ground rules for debate, including no barriers to the thinking. The team challenged their assumptions and in the end developed a means of in-season forecasting that served the new demands. The solution they arrived at started as a wild idea, but with input from IT, it became a plausible reality.

INVESTING IN RENEWABLE ENERGY Gregory Pal is a thoughtful and intense MIT graduate with an MBA from Harvard who works as a manager in an alternative energy start-up. Gregory is known for his ability to solve complex problems. As a reviewer of the early versions of this book, he admitted to feeling torn between his growing desire to lead like a Multiplier and the mounting pressures he faced at work. He found a way through his dilemma by taking on the 30-Day Challenge with a clear and focused target in mind.

Gregory had recently hired Michael, a talented individual with rich experience as an employee of the Brazilian embassy, but wasn't fully utilizing him. Michael was the only team member working remotely and was often "out of sight, out of mind." Michael estimated he was being utilized at the 20 to 25 percent mark.

Gregory began the challenge by making a few simple investments. He gave Michael full ownership for capturing their Brazilian partnership strategy on paper for a critical board meeting. He then integrated Michael virtually into company-wide meetings so his ideas could be heard. He touched base with him often, but didn't take over his work. Within just a couple of weeks, Michael said he felt like he was being utilized at 75 to 80 percent. This represents a threefold utilization gain!

Yet the real gain, according to Gregory, came from a slight change in perspective. Once he started looking at the people around him through the lens of a Multiplier, he said that opportunities started presenting themselves. Instead of feeling frustrated at having to step in and redo work, he found ways to help other people take their thinking to the next level. He could take charge without taking over. He began to do things differently because he began to see his role differently.

Greg McKeown and I have been inspired as we have witnessed senior leaders and front-line managers taking the 30-Day Challenge. It has been interesting to read their journals as they documented their struggles and successes. In many cases these leaders have been generously willing to publish their experiences here and online at www.MultipliersBook.com. Here you can check out their stories, download tools to take the 30-Day Challenge yourself, and share your success. Join the community of leaders taking the Multiplier Challenge.

SUSTAINING MOMENTUM

Taking a 30-Day Challenge will put you on the Multiplier path and will produce initial traction and momentum. But it takes more than a quick win to truly become a Multiplier. Sustaining the momentum takes repetition, time, and reinforcement.

1. BUILD IT LAYER BY LAYER. I remember exactly where I was the first time I heard *Boléro*, the classical music composition by Maurice Ravel. Its stark simplicity and powerful conclusion made a lasting impression on me. The piece, which Ravel himself described as containing almost "no music," is an exploration of repetition and crescendo. It consists of a simple two-part melody repeated eighteen times over the course of fifteen minutes. In each repetition, a new instrument is added as the orchestra plays with increased energy, growing more insistent and louder.[5] It opens simply with two flutes. Then in comes a bassoon. Then another layer is added with a clarinet and then an oboe and next a trumpet. Soon there are strings, woodwinds, and brass to vary the texture of the music. With each new layer of instruments, momentum and energy build. The piece, which began softly with only the sound of a flute, culminates as the entire orchestra sounds the simple theme and ends with a booming crescendo as the last of the 4,037 drumbeats is heard.

Mastery of skills like those of the Multiplier is developed in much the same way that *Boléro* unfolds: a layer at a time, building on a simple tune. A leader begins with a simple assumption and a singular idea, that *people are smart and the job of the leader is to draw out the intelligence of others.* With this simple idea, leaders might begin by restraining themselves more and listening to others. They then might start asking more questions. They become skilled in the art of asking the right questions and begin posing the most difficult questions that challenge the underlying assumptions of the organization. They then use these questions to seed and establish challenges for the organization. Next they bring this sense of challenge and inquiry into key decisions and become masterful Debate Makers. Like the instruments in *Boléro*, by adding these skills a layer at a time, they achieve mastery and have a powerful effect on others.

Becoming a Multiplier is achieved with a single idea, repeated over and over, while new skills are introduced and orchestrated into a leadership gestalt.

2. STAY WITH IT FOR A YEAR. Momentum can be built quickly. Mastery takes time. In his book *Outliers*, Malcolm Gladwell introduces the "10,000-Hour Rule" citing the research of Anders Ericsson and others that claims that the development of expertise or greatness is a function of practice and time—about 10,000 hours of practice, to be exact. While true mastery indeed develops over years of regular practice, a foundation or baseline of capability can be established in one year of consistent, purposeful effort.

An insightful colleague, Dinesh Chandra, once observed that the best work is done when one can hold a single question for a long time. Dinesh is known for asking, "What is the question that you are asking yourself this year?" Each year, he carries with him a question that challenges his thinking and sparks learning. Inspired by Dinesh a couple of years ago, I adopted an intriguing question for myself: *How is what I know getting in the way of what I don't know?* By simply asking this question, I was compelled to venture beyond the realm of my own understanding. Holding this question for a year (actually, I'm still working on it) and asking it in numerous settings has helped me transcend the limitations of my own knowledge and find ways to better see and access the intelligence of others.

In the spirit of the Multiplier, one might adopt an annual question, such as:

- What would cause other people to become smarter and more capable around me?

- What could people figure out on their own if I just gave them more space?

- How can I get the full brainpower of my team or organization?

Or simply . . .

- How can I multiply the intelligence of others?

Asking these questions once or twice is interesting. Continuing to ask them again and again during the course of a year (or longer) creates deep learning and builds the hours of practice necessary to achieve mastery.

3. BUILD A COMMUNITY. When three friends decided they all wanted to earn a black belt in judo, they enthusiastically signed up for the challenge together and agreed to rotate driving each other to the gym. But as the week-in and week-out training relentlessly continued, their motivation waned. Despite the pull to quit, all three continued with their training, reaching black belt status together. Their explanation was simple: Each week at least one person didn't feel like going, but no one wanted to let the others down.

Positive peer pressure is a powerful way to sustain momentum in any endeavor. It is, in its own right, a lazy way idea for becoming a Multiplier. The most successful participants of the 30-Day Challenge have worked collectively or have had a partner who served as both a sounding board and accountability point.

Experiment with the power of community in your own organization as a way to spark and sustain momentum. You might start small by finding a couple of colleagues or friends who read this book and want to take the challenge. You might then create an online learning community. Or you may choose to join a community of leaders around the world who aspire to lead like a Multiplier. I have often wondered what type of online community a team of Multipliers would create. How would they make it safe for people to share their best thinking and their boldest ideas? How would challenges get established and how would debate happen? How would this community attract and develop talent and share ownership? By joining forces with a community, you need not have all the answers, or even all the questions. You can look to the genius of the group to guide you.

THE MULTIPLIER EFFECT REVISITED

When Greg and I teach the Multiplier ideas to teams and organizations, we often ask the question, "Does any of this matter?" How does leading like a Multiplier matter to you, to your organization, or even to the world at large? Let us consider each in turn.

First, it matters to you because people will give you more. The research showed consistently that even high-performing people gave Multipliers 2X more than they gave their Diminisher counterparts. People don't give a little more—they give a lot more. They give all of their discretionary effort and mental energy. They dig deep and access reserves of brainpower that they alone know exist. They apply the full measure of their intelligence. They reason more clearly, comprehend more completely, and learn more quickly. In the process they get smarter and more capable.

Your people will give you more, and in return they get a richly satisfying experience. "Exhausting but exhilarating" captures what people continually told us it was like to work for a Multiplier. One woman said, "It was exhausting but I was always ready to do it again. It is not a burnout experience—it is a build-up experience." As you become more of a Multiplier, people will flock to you because you will be "the boss to work for." You will become a Talent Magnet, drawing in and developing talent while providing extraordinary returns to the company as well as to the individuals who work for you.

Second, it matters to the organization you work for. Many

organizations face the double whammy of new challenges and insufficient resources. Perhaps you can relate to one start-up that experienced years of extraordinary growth. Their strategy had been to "throw
people at the problem." But as their growth declined, they had to try
to outperform their market without adding headcount. Suddenly resource leverage was as strategically important as resource allocation. A
leader in a Fortune 500 company recently shared with us that in one
particular division, one in three of his people was utilized below the 20
percent level! Organizations led by Multipliers can more than double
the capability of their people and hence their organizations.

This is a particularly timely message. In down markets and times
of scarcity, managers must find ways to get more capability and productivity from their current resources. Corporations and organizations need managers who can migrate from the logic of addition,
where more resources are required to handle the increased demands,
to a logic of multiplication, where leaders can more fully extract the
capability of their current resources. Resource leverage has the power
of relevancy. It is timely. But it is also timeless.

It is timeless because even in times of abundance and growth, companies need leaders who can multiply the intelligence and capability
of their colleagues and increase the brainpower of the organization to
meet its growth demands. In down markets or growth markets, leading like a Multiplier matters to the organization you work for.

Third, leading like a Multiplier matters to the world at large.
Albert Einstein is credited with saying, "The significant problems we
face cannot be solved at the same level of thinking we were at when
we created them." But what if we could access twice as much of the
available intelligence and channel it to the perennial problems we
face? What solutions could we generate if we could access the underutilized brainpower in the world? Surely we need leaders who can
extract and utilize all available intelligence to solve our most complex and vital challenges. Leading like a Multiplier matters to the
world at large.

GENIUS OR GENIUS MAKER?

When Philippe Petit illegally connected a tightrope wire between the 1,368-foot Twin Towers in New York City, he still had the chance to change his mind. The moment of truth came later, when he stood with one foot still on the building and another on the wire in front of him. The wire was bouncing up and down from the airflow between the buildings. His weight was still on his back leg. Recall once more how Petit described that critical moment as he stood on the edge overlooking the chasm. He reflected, "I had to make a decision of shifting my weight from one foot anchored to the building to the foot anchored on the wire. Something I could not resist called me [out] on that cable." He shifted his weight and took the first step.

At the conclusion of this book, you may feel like Petit, with one foot anchored to the building of the status quo and the other anchored to the wire of change. You can remove your foot from the wire, lean back, and continue to lead the way you have in the past. Or you can shift your weight onto the wire and lead more like a Multiplier. Inertia will keep you on the building where it is comfortable and safe. But for many of us there is also a force pulling us out onto the wire and to a more impactful and fulfilling way of leading others. Will you shift your weight?

Consider some of the Multipliers who have made it across:

- Entrepreneurs Thomas and Andreas Strüengmann, who built billions of dollars of value in their company on their ability to find and develop the natural genius in others

- History teacher Patrick Kelly, who creates an environment that draws out his students' very best thinking and work, and whose 98 percent of students score at the proficient or advanced levels on state tests

- Nobel Laureate Wangari Maathai, who started small by planting seven seedling trees but eventually created an irresistible challenge that resulted in 40 million trees being planted across Africa

- Activist Ela Bhatt, SEWA founder (and now member of the esteemed group, The Elders, established by Nelson Mandela), who built up leaders to fully own and guide organizations she began

Leading like a Multiplier is a choice we encounter daily or perhaps in every moment. What choices are you making? And how will these choices affect what the people around you become? Is it possible that the choice you make about how you lead can impact not just your team, or even your immediate sphere of influence, but generations to come? A single Accidental Diminisher turned Multiplier could have a profound and far-reaching impact in a world where the challenges are so great and our full intelligence underutilized.

It seems possible that there are Diminisher assumptions holding whole businesses back. What could happen if one aspiring Multiplier introduced people around them to these ideas? What would happen if an organization currently operating on 50 percent of its intelligence moved to the 100 percent level? When Accidental Diminishers become Multipliers, they are like Sir Galahad, whose "strength was as the strength of ten." This is because Multipliers are the key to everyone else's intelligence. A Multiplier is the key to unlocking capability. A single Multiplier matters.

It is plausible that Diminisher assumptions are underlying failing schools. What would transpire at a school if one principal learned to lead like a Multiplier and found a way to give teachers, parents, and students greater ownership for the success of the school? What if these students and teachers learned these principles together? What would happen to families if parents led like Multipliers in their homes?

Many governments are suffocating, even collapsing. Is it possible for our civic leaders to seed challenges and then turn to the community for answers? Could answers to our most vexing challenges be found through rigorous debate and the extraction of the full intelligence of the community? Could Diminishing leaders be replaced by those who serve as true Multipliers, inspiring collective intelligence and capability on a mass scale?

I believe that the Diminishing cultures we see in organizations, schools, and even families are not inevitable. Indeed, in the last analysis, Diminishing cultures may simply be unsustainable. To the extent that these cultures are based on incorrect assumptions, they will violate the truth about how people work and thrive. Like many historical empires, they will eventually collapse. It may be that the only institutions that will be left standing in turbulent times are those that harvest the abundance of intelligence available to them and operate on correct assumptions.

We began this inquiry with an intriguing observation about two political leaders paraphrased by Bono, the rock star and global activist. He said, "It has been said that after meeting with the great British Prime Minister William Ewart Gladstone, you left feeling he was the smartest person in the world, but after meeting with his rival Benjamin Disraeli, you left thinking you were the smartest person."[6] The observation captures the essence and the power of a Multiplier.

Which will you be: A genius? Or a genius maker? Perhaps, you stand with one foot on the building and the other on the wire. The choice matters.

BECOMING A MULTIPLIER

THE LAZY WAY STRATEGY

Use the right principles and tools and attain maximum results with just the right amount of effort.

The Accelerators

1. *Work the Extremes:* Assess your leadership practices and then focus your development on the two extremes: 1) bring up your lowest low and 2) take your highest high to the next level.

2. *Start with the Assumptions:* Adopt the assumptions of a Multiplier and allow the behavior and practices to naturally follow.

- *If I can find someone's genius, I can put them to work.*
- *People's best thinking must be given, not taken.*
- *People get smarter by being challenged.*
- *With enough minds, we can figure it out.*
- *People are smart and will figure things out.*

3. *Take a 30-Day Multiplier Challenge:* Pick one practice within one discipline, and work it for thirty days.

Sustaining Momentum

1. Build it layer by layer.

2. Stay with it for a year.

3. Build a community.

ACKNOWLEDGMENTS

It should be obvious by now that this book is the work of many people, not just one or two. We are indebted to so many and would like to thank everyone who has offered their insights and put their thumbprint on this work.

The first group is perhaps the least obvious but most essential: the nominators—the original people we interviewed who told us of their experiences working with the Multipliers and Diminishers throughout their careers. The witness protection program requires that we don't list their names, but they know who they are. This book exists because they have shared their experiences and insights. Of course, there are the Multipliers who allowed us to study them and who have shared their stories. There is a listing of these Multipliers in Appendix C. These leaders, and the other rock stars whose stories we couldn't fit into the book, were our constant inspiration. It is our hope that their way of leadership inspires countless more leaders like them.

Next, the book was made stronger by a team of reviewers who read early versions of the book and helped us polish the ideas. Your comments both kept us on track and kept us going. A big shout out goes to: Evette Allen, Shannon Colquhoun, Sally Crawford, Margie Duffy, Peter Fortenbaugh, Holly Goodliffe, Sebastian Gunningham, Ranu Gupta,

John Hall, Kirsten Hansen, Jade Koyle, Matt Macauley, Stu Maclennan, Justin McKeown, Sue Nelson, Todd Paletta, Ben Putterman, Gordon Rudow, Stefan Schaffer, Lisa Shiveley, Stan Slap, Hilary Somorjai, John Somorjai, Fronda Stringer Wiseman, Ilana Tandowsky, Guryan Tighe, Mike Thornberry, Jake White, Alan Wilkins, Beth Wilkins, John Wiseman, Britton Worthen, and Bruce and Pam Worthen.

There were several people who went so far and above the role of reviewer that we need to scream out a special thank you to them. These folks gave us new ideas, interesting stories, voluntary rewrites, plus good old-fashioned moral support. If there was a crime scene investigation, the following people would have more than thumbprints on the work—their DNA would be all over it: Jesse Anderson, Heidi Brandow, Amy Hayes Stellhorn, Matt Lobaugh, Greg Pal, Gadi Shamia, and Kristine Westerlind. And I owe a particular debt to my mother and on-demand editor, Lois Allen. She pretended this was just another high school term paper and reviewed every word and fixed countless errors so others could review the ideas without being distracted. Mom, you continue to make me better.

We were fortunate to land with a highly experienced and collaborative publishing team at HarperCollins. As a first-time author, I kept waiting to get beat up, but instead, we were built up. This was made possible by our insightful editor, Hollis Heimbouch. Hollis, thank you for "getting it" instantly, for guiding us, and for so deeply embracing what it means to be a Multiplier in your own work. And thanks go to Matthew Inman and the team at HarperCollins for your diligent labors on behalf of this book. To Shannon Marven, our agent at Dupree-Miller, thanks for signing up with us, for your tenacity, and for making this all possible (and for making my kids think I'm way cool for having an agent).

There are a few people whose role has been much broader than just this book that I must acknowledge. I have been fortunate to have many great mentors who have let me borrow their minds and see the world through their most brilliant lens. Here are a few who have shaped my views and who have influenced this book profoundly. Dr. C.K. Prahalad, the great management thinker, who taught me the importance of reaching deep into an organization for intelligence and how to build collective intent. C.K., thank you for encouraging these ideas, for helping us unearth the core assumptions, and for guiding the book in many ways. I have always been proud just to be your student. Dr. J. Bonnor Ritchie, professor and peace broker, who early on shared with me (and each of his students) his insatiable intellectual curiosity and inspired us to truly embrace ambiguity. Ray Lane, the extraordinary business leader, who taught me how to lead, and who was a Multiplier to me and so many others. Kerry Patterson, the writer and great teacher, who raised our sights and encouraged us to write this book not just for corporate managers but for leaders all across the world. Kerry, thank you for coaching and pushing me harder, even when it involved a good beating.

Lastly, this book is a result of two enduring partnerships for which I am both privileged and grateful. Greg McKeown, my research and thought partner, for his fanatical need for clarity and his relentless pursuit of truth in all he does. Thank you for joining me on this journey, for setting the aspiration level high, and for sharing your genius. Anna, thank you for sharing Greg.

My deepest appreciation goes to my husband, Larry, for believing in this project from day one, for guarding my space to work on it like a watch dog, and for making me feel like a genius every day of my life.

To each of the above, thank you for so generously contributing your time and energy in bringing forward these ideas. We hope that we have done justice to what you've given us.

THE RESEARCH PROCESS

In this appendix you will find a detailed account of the research Greg and I conducted to study the differences between Diminishers and Multipliers. We will outline the research process in three phases: 1) the foundation work for the research; 2) the research itself; and 3) the development of the Multiplier model.

PHASE 1: THE FOUNDATION

RESEARCH TEAM While Greg and I were the primary members of the research team, C.K. Prahalad served as an important, informal research advisor. While many people contributed to the research in the book, our core was as follows:

Liz Wiseman, Master of Organizational Behavior, Marriott School of Management, Brigham Young University

Greg McKeown, Master of Business Administration, Stanford Graduate School of Business

C.K. Prahalad, Paul and Ruth McCracken Distinguished University Professor of Corporate Strategy at the Ross School of Business of the University of Michigan

RESEARCH QUESTION Through an iterative process we refined our research questions as: "What are the vital few differences between intelligence Diminishers and intelligence Multipliers, and what impact do they have on organizations?"

Inherent in this question was the idea of contrast. We reasoned that it wasn't enough to study Multipliers. As Jim Collins has explained, if you only studied gold medalists at the Olympics, you might erroneously conclude that they won because they all had coaches. It is only by contrasting winners with the people who lost that you realize that everyone has a coach, so having a coach cannot be the active ingredient in winning.[1] We were looking for the active ingredients or differentiating factors.

DEFINITION OF KEY TERMS To be able to answer our research question we defined our three key terms: Diminisher, Multiplier, and intelligence.

DIMINISHER: a person who led an organization or management team that operated in silos, found it hard to get things done, and despite having smart people, seemed to not be able to do what it needed to do to reach its goals.

MULTIPLIER: a person who led an organization or management team that was able to understand and solve hard problems rapidly, achieve its goals, and adapt and increase its capacity over time.

INTELLIGENCE: In our literature review we found a paper that identified more than seventy definitions of intelligence.[2] One paper that was important to us throughout the research process was signed by fifty-two researchers in 1994. They agreed that intelligence was "the ability to reason, plan, solve problems, think abstractly, comprehend complex ideas, learn quickly and learn from experience. It is not . . . narrow. . . . [I]t is a broader and deeper capability for comprehending our surroundings— 'catching on,' 'making sense' of things, or 'figuring out' what to do."[3] Beyond this, we included the ability to adapt to new environments, learn new skills, and accomplish difficult tasks.

INDUSTRY SELECTION Having first observed the Diminisher/Multiplier phenomenon at Oracle, a software company, we opted to research the phenomenon in other companies within the broader technology industry. These companies included:

Technology Industry	Company
Biotech	Affymetrix
Online Retailing	Amazon
Consumer Electronics	Apple
Networking and Communications	Cisco
Internet Search	Google
Microprocessors	Intel
Computer Software	Microsoft
Enterprise Software Applications	SAP

PHASE 2: THE RESEARCH

NOMINATORS Instead of trying to identify Diminishers and Multipliers ourselves, we found people who would nominate these leaders for us. We used two criteria in the selection of our nominators. The first was that they should be successful professionals. It was important that these individuals had positive career experiences to draw from. We reasoned that interviewing people who had "an axe to grind" could skew the data.

The second criteria was that these nominators have approximately ten years' management experience themselves. We wanted practical insight from people who had grappled with challenges of leading others. It is worth noting that nominators at many of the above companies pointed us to both Multipliers and Diminishers they had worked with at entirely different companies and often industries.

RESEARCHER-ADMINISTERED SURVEY We asked the nominators to rate the Multipliers and Diminishers they had identified on a five-point scale against forty-eight leadership practices. We designed the list to be comprehensive, drawing upon standard competency models, popular leadership frameworks, and practices we hypothesized would differentiate Diminishers from Multipliers.

The survey included *skills* (e.g., "Focuses on the customer"; "Demonstrates intellectual curiosity"; "Develops the talent of the team"; and "Business acumen") and *mindsets* (e.g., "See their role as a primary thought leader" and "See intelligence as continually developing"). We collected the results of this survey and analyzed the data in several ways. We looked for the largest deltas between Multipliers and Diminishers, the top skills and mindsets of Multipliers, and the skills most correlated with the top mindsets of Multipliers and Diminishers.

STRUCTURED INTERVIEWS In the original interviews with the nominators, we followed a structured format. We used the same questions in the same order to minimize context effects, or at least hold them constant, so we could ensure reliable aggregation and comparison of the answers we received across different interviews and timeframes.

All the interviews were conducted between October 2007 and October 2009, with the first round of interviews transpiring in 2007. The interviews averaged between sixty and ninety minutes and were conducted in-person or by telephone. We kept written transcripts of all the conversations so we would have a permanent record of quotations and examples. While we followed a structured format, we allowed

THE RESEARCH PROCESS

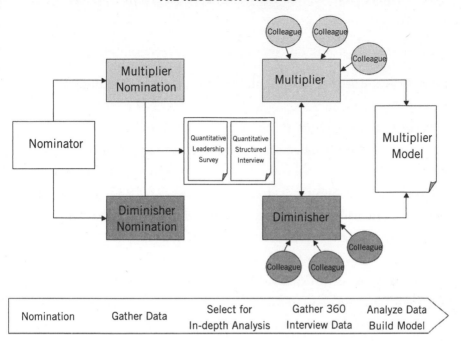

ourselves some latitude in determining how much time to devote to each question. Our typical format for an interview kept to the following narrative structure:

1. Identification of two leaders: one who stifled intelligence and the other who amplified it

2. Identification of an experience or story working with each leader

3. Context for working with Diminisher: experience, setting

4. Impact on nominator: percentage of nominator's capability used

5. Impact on group: role played in group process, perception in broader organization

6. Leader's actions: what was done or not done to impact others

7. Result of actions: outcomes, deliverables accomplished

8. Repeat questions 3 through 7 for the nominated Multiplier

STRUCTURED INTERVIEWS: FOLLOW-UP We conducted a second round of interviews to gather more information about the strongest Multipliers. This included: a) interviews with the Multipliers themselves; b) second interviews with the nominators to gather greater detail and understanding; and c) an in-depth 360 process interviewing both former and current members of the Multiplier's management team.

INDUSTRY EXPANSION As we extended our research to eventually include 144 different leaders, we found more examples within our original target companies, added more companies within the technology and biotech industries, and went beyond these industries entirely to include others in the for-profit sector as well as nonprofits and government agencies. Our research journey took us across four continents and introduced us to a rich and diverse set of leaders (see Appendix C). The following is a list of organizations where we studied Multipliers. In order to provide confidentiality, we are not publishing the list of companies where we studied Diminishers.

Industry	Example Companies
Biotech	Hexal, Affymetrix
Green Tech	Bloom Energy, Better Place
Education	Stanford University, VitalSmarts
Entertainment	DreamWorks Studios
Government	White House, Israeli Army
Manufacturing	GM Daewoo, Flextronics

Industry	Example Companies
Nonprofit	Boys and Girls Club of the Peninsular, Green Belt Movement, Bennion Center, Unitus
Private Equity and Venture Capitalists	Advent International, Kleiner Perkins Caulfield & Byers
Professional Services	Bain & Company, McKinsey & Company
Retailing	Gap, Lands End, Gymboree
Sports	Highland High School Rugby, North Carolina State University women's basketball program
Technology Industry	Amazon, Apple, Cisco, Infosys Technologies, Hewlett Packard, Intel, Intuit, Microsoft, SAP, Salesforce.com
Workers' Union	Self-Employed Women's Association

PHASE 3: THE MODEL

We gathered approximately 400 pages of interview transcripts, read them multiple times, and collated them for cross-interview analysis. We then took this theme analysis and calibrated it against the quantitative data we had gathered from the leadership survey. Finally, we adhered to a disciplined and rigorous debate methodology for crafting each of the disciplines that eventually became chapters for the book.

Both Greg and I claim to have been severely beaten up by each other during this debate process. We hope the research is stronger for it.

FREQUENTLY ASKED QUESTIONS

ARE PEOPLE EITHER DIMINISHERS OR MULTIPLIERS OR ARE THERE PEOPLE IN THE MIDDLE?

We see the Diminisher–Multiplier model as a continuum with a few people at the extremes and most of us somewhere in between. As people have been introduced to this material, they almost always see some of the Diminisher and some of the Multiplier within themselves. One leader we've worked with is illustrative. He was a smart and aware individual who didn't fit the archetype of a Diminisher, and yet when he read the material he could see how he sometimes behaved in a Diminishing manner. While we studied this leadership phenomenon as a contrast, we see the model as a continuum with only a very few people at the polar extremes and the majority of us somewhere in the middle.

CAN EVERYONE BECOME A MULTIPLIER OR ARE THERE SOME PEOPLE WHO ARE TOO MUCH OF A DIMINISHER TO CHANGE?

Anyone who can see their Diminisher behavior can change. Anyone can be a Multiplier if they're willing to shift their center of weight and look beyond themselves. There may be a few people who are so staunchly invested in their Diminisher approach to leadership that they won't be able to change, but we think of them as outliers.

In our work teaching and coaching, we have seen people make

significant changes. For example, one leader we worked with had some strong Diminisher tendencies. He worked hard to adopt a more Multiplier approach to his leadership. People noticed the difference. Then, after he took a larger role at another company, he was able to start with a clean slate and a new approach. He is now seen as a Multiplier and has even introduced these ideas to the people in his organization.

We aren't under the delusion that every Diminisher *will* change, but we believe that the vast majority can make the shift. It begins with awareness and intent.

SHOULD COMPANIES FIRE THEIR DIMINISHERS?

Smart companies don't have to fire every Diminisher, but they should remove them from key leadership roles. If someone insists on being a Diminisher, they may need to be isolated or contained where they can't do great damage. If they are removed from key leadership roles, other people's capability gets released and the Diminishers are less likely to inspire managers underneath them to adopt Diminishing leadership practices.

This is easier said than done. Diminishers are, by definition, smart and intimidating. The course of least resistance is to keep them in their leadership roles. But once you start to calculate the high cost of Diminishers in your organization, you will be better prepared to take action. For example, if you had a machine that was a bottleneck causing the rest of your production line to operate at 50 percent capacity, you would see immediately how expensive that machine was to your operation. If you replaced that one machine you could double the capacity and throughput of your entire production line! That is what is at stake with every Diminisher you have in a key leadership role. Even if they are operating at full capacity, they operate as a bottleneck to everyone else around them. So while the answer may not be to fire every Diminisher, we suggest that it's just too expensive to leave them in key leadership roles.

ARE THERE TIMES WHEN DIMINISHER LEADERSHIP IS CALLED FOR?

Yes, there probably are times when the Diminisher approach is justi-
fied, but they are few and far between. If you can honestly say that you
can afford for your people to operate at 50 percent of their capacity,
that there is an impending crisis, that your insight is genuinely and
significantly greater than the people around you, and that there is no
reasonable chance that others could get up to speed quickly enough,
then the Diminisher approach may be the right approach. By paral-
lel, if your child is running into the street, any number of Diminisher
practices are reasonable and advisable.

In allowing for this, we would still emphasize that most situations,
even extreme ones, can be viewed through either a Diminisher or
Multiplier lens. Situations people often think call for a Diminisher approach can be exactly the time to call upon the full intellectual horsepower of the people around you. When the stakes are high, when the
challenges are complex and nonlinear, that may be just the time when
the Multiplier approach is most relevant.

There are times when every leader may, in good conscience, operate as a Diminisher. We advise keeping those moments to a minimum.
These can and should be extreme exceptions to the rule.

**WHEN YOU SAY MULTIPLIERS GET 2X MORE FROM THEIR PEOPLE, THAT SEEMS LIKE
A REALLY BIG CLAIM. IS IT REALLY THAT MUCH?**

Yes, the number seemed high to us at first, but for several reasons we
believe the ratio is correct.

First, we asked the nominators to contrast Multipliers *to Diminishers*, rather than contrasting Multipliers to an average manager. The 2X
effect assumes a best-to-worst comparison. Second, we repeated this
question to people across industry, function, and management level
and have confirmation that this ratio holds true as an average. Third,
the surprisingly high difference may be the result of discretionary
effort. As managers we can observe whether someone is working at,
above, or below their usual productivity level. What is harder to know

is how much a person is holding back. The way people answer this question suggests that people believe they hold back a considerable amount around certain managers.

We have concluded that while it is an amazing difference, Multipliers really do get, on average, 2X more than their Diminisher counterparts.

ISN'T THIS JUST ENLIGHTENED LEADERSHIP WITH A NEW NAME?

The Multiplier model is more than just enlightened leadership. Sure, it is enlightened in that it benefits the people who work around Multipliers and get to work at their highest point of contribution and thrive. But the Multiplier model is also a practical approach to management because Multipliers get more from the people they lead—much more. They get more intelligent action, more adroit problem solving, and more concentrated effort. While that might seem "enlightened" it is also just a practical and productive way to lead.

ARE MULTIPLIERS MORE SUCCESSFUL THAN DIMINISHERS?

Yes, they are more successful *at getting more out of people*. This was amazingly consistent throughout our research. Even high-powered executives, icons in their own right, who hammered their people simply could not get as much out of people as their Multiplier counterparts. We didn't study the career trajectories of Diminishers and Multipliers themselves, but we did study the success of the people they worked around. We found that people and their careers thrived and became more successful around Multipliers than around Diminishers.

HOW DO THESE DYNAMICS CHANGE ACROSS CULTURES?

The international research we have done thus far confirms that this model is relevant and recognizable across continents and cultures. There is more research that could be done to verify this and to look for the subtle differences. We do find that some national cultures have inherent Diminisher tendencies and a management legacy built on

Diminisher assumptions and practices. But in the original research and the subsequent teaching of this material we have found almost universal resonance.

THERE ARE SOME LEADERS YOU MENTION WHOM YOU HAVE IDENTIFIED AS MULTIPLIERS, BUT WHO ARE SOMETIMES KNOWN TO DIMINISH THE PEOPLE THEY WORK WITH. HOW DO YOU EXPLAIN THE CONTRADICTION?

Yes, this was interesting to us, too. Even in our original data pool, we occasionally found that some leaders were named as both a Diminisher and a Multiplier by different people. On closer inspection, we found this to be a paradox rather than a contradiction. As just one illustration, we found that some leaders had figured out how to involve their direct reports, but hadn't learned to scale their leadership to the broader organization. The farther removed people were from the leader, the more diminished they felt. It was a classic case of Accidental Diminishing. It appears that being a Multiplier to *everyone* takes deliberate intention and effort. A leader needs to think consciously of the people at the periphery of the organization in order to be a Multiplier to them.

DID YOU ANSWER THE QUESTION YOU SET OUT TO?

Yes, but it has raised other questions.

Along the way, as any good researchers should, we have found ourselves asking new and related questions. One question is: How can you create a Multiplier culture in an organization (business, hospital, school)? We studied leaders who have already created such a climate, but what if someone is starting from scratch? We have some experience with this, but we hope with further work and study to be able to answer it with more rigor.

A second question this research has raised is: Why are some people never diminished? This is fascinating to us. Some people showed up in our research as being relatively immune to Diminishers. They appear to be able to turn any situation into one they can learn from and thrive in. They appear somewhat invincible or unbreakable. We think this might deserve a more serious examination.

We have answered our original question to our own satisfaction, but we have found that it has raised new questions for us. We are eager to dig into these new questions.

DO YOU HAVE TO INTRODUCE THESE IDEAS AT THE TOP OF AN ORGANIZATION?

It is easiest to drive wide-scale change by starting at the top. However, you can still begin within your own team. If the CEO is on board, that is to your advantage, but it isn't necessary. You can begin where you are, make your team a success story, and build momentum from there. In every organization we studied we found leaders who created Multiplier cultures, even without top-level support and often in Diminishing cultures. We recently worked with a team who had spent several years being diminished by their CEO. But as they became aware of their own management choices, they realized they could start where they were. They could make Multiplier choices. If you can get executive sponsorship, it will be to your advantage. But you can start with your own team, learn what works, and then involve other people from the broader organization.

SHOULD I EVEN TRY TO HAND THIS BOOK TO A RAGING DIMINISHER?

Yes, drop it and run! Or perhaps you can send it from one of your other Diminsher colleagues!

More seriously, if you share the book from a Diminisher's perspective, by judging and dictating, you are likely to close down the person and continue the Diminishing cycle. However, if you approach it as a Multiplier, and make it safe for someone to learn new ideas, you might find surprising levels of receptiveness and impact. Here are two Multiplier strategies:

1. Focus on your own experience. You might begin by acknowledging how each of us can be an Accidental Diminisher at times and say something like, "This book has shown me how

I sometimes diminish people without meaning to." Or you can focus on the impact it has had for you and introduce it with, "I've been working on being more of a Multiplier and I'm seeing how it is increasing performance on my team. I thought you might be interested, too."

2. Focus on the upside to the organization. Most managers would be interested in doubling the capacity of their organization. You could introduce the ideas with, "I think we have more intelligence in our organization than we've been able to tap into. I think there are some things that we could do as a leadership team to raise the IQ level of our organization."

3. Additionally, you could introduce the ideas indirectly by holding a brown-bag lunch discussion or by sharing a single idea or Multiplier practice. We believe that there is a way to share this material with almost anyone, but you are more likely to succeed if you approach it like a Multiplier. You can't diminish people into being Multipliers!

IF I COULD DO ONE THING TO GET ON THE PATH OF MULTIPLIER, WHAT SHOULD IT BE?
The one thing we would suggest you do is to ask really insightful and interesting questions that make people think. This is a practical step and it applies across all of the disciplines. For example, whether you are trying to become a Liberator or a Challenger or a Debate Maker, asking insightful and interesting questions will get you started down the correct path. So if you are looking to build one skill, start with questions.

If you want to work on one assumption, we would suggest trying on "people are smart and will figure it out." One way to do this is ask the question, "How is this person smart?" Asking that question can interrupt any tendencies to judge people in a binary fashion. It can work like a fast-pass into the Technicolor world where Multipliers live.

THE MULTIPLIERS

The following is a list of the "Hall of Fame" Multipliers featured in this book. Several appear in multiple chapters, but they are listed only once below in the chapter that they are featured in most prominently.

Multiplier	Featured Role	Current Role
Chapter 1: The Multiplier Effect		
Lior	Company Commander, Israeli Army	
George Schneer	Division Manager, Intel	Executive-in-Residence, Sevin Rosen Funds; Partner, Horizon Ventures
Tim Cook	COO, Apple Inc.	COO, Apple Inc.
Deborah Lange	SVP, Taxation, Oracle Corporation	Retired
George Clooney	Actor	Actor; Activist
Chapter 2: The Talent Magnet		
Mitt Romney	Consulting Manager, Bain & Company	Political Leader
Andreas Strüengmann	Cofounder, Hexal, Germany	Executive, Sandoz (Generics Division of Novartis); Billionaire Investor

Multiplier	Featured Role	Current Role
Thomas Strüengmann	Cofounder, Hexal, Germany	Board of Directors Novartis; Billionaire Investor
Zvi Schreiber	CEO, G.ho.st, Israel and Palestine	CEO, G.ho.st, Israel and Palestine
Larry Gelwix	Head Coach, Highland High School Rugby	Head Coach, Highland High School Rugby
Marguerite Gong Hancock	Girls' Camp Director	Associate Director, Stanford Program on Regions of Innovation and Entrepreneurship
K.R. Sridhar	CEO, Bloom Energy	CEO, Bloom Energy
Chapter 3: The Liberator		
Robert Enslin	President, SAP North America	President, SAP North America
Ernest Bachrach	Managing Partner, Advent International, Latin America	Chief Executive, Advent International, Latin America
Steven Spielberg	Film Director	Film Director
Patrick Kelly	8th-Grade Social Studies and History Teacher	8th-Grade Social Studies and History Teacher
Ray Lane	President, Oracle	Partner, Kleiner Perkins Caufield & Byers Venture Capital
John Brandon	Vice President, Channel Sales, Apple Inc.	Vice President, Channel and Commercial Sales, Apple Inc.
Nick Reilly	CEO, GM Daewoo, Korea	Executive Vice President, General Motors Co.
Alan G. Lafley	CEO, Procter & Gamble	Coauthor, *The Game Changer*
Chapter 4: The Challenger		
Shai Agassi	CEO, Better Place; Executive Vice President, SAP	CEO, Better Place

Multiplier	Featured Role	Current Role
Irene Fisher	Director, Bennion Center	Former Founder/Director, University Neighbor Partners; Community Activist
C.K. Prahalad	Professor, University of Michigan	Professor, University of Michigan
Matt McCauley	CEO, Gymboree	CEO, Gymboree
Sean Mendy	Director, Center for the New Generation, Boys and Girls Club of the Peninsula	Stanford University Graduate Student; Director, Center for the New Generation,, Boys and Girls Club of the Peninsula
Wangari Maathai	Founder, Green Belt Movement, Africa	2004 Laureate, Nobel Prize for Peace
Chapter 5: The Debate Maker		
Barack Obama	President-Elect, United States of America	President, United States of America
Lutz Ziob	GM, Microsoft Learning, Microsoft Corporation	GM, Microsoft Learning, Microsoft Corporation
Tim Brown	CEO and President, IDEO	CEO and President, IDEO
Sue Siegel	President, Affymetrix	Partner, Mohr Davidow Ventures
Chapter 6: The Investor		
Jae Choi	Partner, McKinsey & Company, Korea	Executive Managing Director, Doosan, Korea
Elaben Bhatt	Founder, SEWA, India	Member, The Elders World Council
John Chambers	CEO, Cisco Systems	CEO, Cisco Systems
Michael Clark	Division President, Flextronics	Division President, Flextronics
John Wookey	Executive Vice President, Oracle; Executive Vice President, SAP	Executive Vice President, SAP
Kerry Patterson	Cofounder, Interact Performance Systems	Author; Cofounder, VitalSmarts

Multiplier	Featured Role	Current Role
Jubin Dana	Coach, California Youth Soccer Association	Coach, California Youth Soccer Association; Lawyer
Narayana Murthy	CEO, Infosys, India	Nonexecutive Chairman, Chief Mentor, Infosys; Political and Business Thought Leader, India
Chapter 7: Becoming a Multiplier		
Bill Campbell	CEO, Intuit	Chairman, Intuit; Advisor to Silicon Valley CEOs

MULTIPLIERS DISCUSSION GUIDE

This guide contains a set of questions for discussing Multiplier ideas as a team. As you plan your discussions, you might look for ways to create a Multiplier experience while discussing Multiplier ideas.

Chapter	Discussion Questions
The Multiplier Effect	■ Should a successful Diminisher try to become a Multiplier? Why? ■ Can you be a Multiplier if you work for a Diminisher? ■ Are there certain people who bring out the Diminisher in you? Why?
Talent Magnet	■ How long does it take to develop a reputation as "the boss to work for"? ■ When should you hire new people versus develop the talent of the people you already have?
Liberator	■ A liberating climate gives a lot of space and expects a lot at the same time. How do you know when you have gone too far with either element?

Chapter	Discussion Questions
	■ Does being a Liberator mean you have to be both "loathed and loved" the way Mr. Kelly is at his school? (See page 75)
Challenger	■ How can you share your own knowledge and opinions without diminishing the people you lead? ■ What one thing could Richard Palmer do to shift from leading like a Diminisher to leading like a Multiplier? (See page 100)
Debate Maker	■ Imagine you have only thirty minutes to make a high-stakes decision. Should you still approach the decision as a Debate Maker? If no, why? If yes, how? ■ Being a Debate Maker means driving sound decisions through a rigorous process. How do you know when there has been enough debate and it is time to make a decision?
Investor	■ What is the difference between being detail oriented and micromanaging? ■ How can you give people full ownership without becoming disengaged yourself?
Becoming a Multiplier	■ If you had to define one idea that is common across all five disciplines, what would it be? ■ What discipline could you make the most progress on in the least amount of time? ■ Is it feasible to focus on a single area of development for a year? ■ Where is your weight on the metaphorical wire? (see page 220)

Chapter	Discussion Questions
	■ Of the various organizations you are part of (business, community, family), where could you implement the Multiplier approach with the greatest impact? Why?

If you'd like to lead a more structured event, you can download a full Multipliers Facilitator Guide at www.multipliersbook.com. Use it to bring Multiplier leadership into the conversation at your workplace!

THE MULTIPLIERS ASSESSMENT

Are You an Accidental Diminisher?

In our research, we were surprised to discover how few Diminishers understood the restrictive impact they were having on others. Most had moved into management, having been praised for their personal—and often intellectual—merit and had assumed their role as boss was to have the best ideas. Others had once had the mind of a Multiplier, but had been working among Diminishers for so long, they had gone native.

Accidental or not, the impact on your team is the same—you might be getting only one-half of the true brainpower of your team.

The Accidental Diminisher Quiz is a quick assessment that will allow you to

- Reflect on 10 common management scenarios and how closely they describe your own approach to management.

- See to what extent you may be inadvertently diminishing your people. You'll get an instant "A.D. Score" (the smaller, the better)!

- Get an immediate report analyzing your responses with suggestions for how you can adjust your leadership practices to lead more like a Multiplier and get more from your team.

To access the Accidental Diminisher Quiz, go to
www.multipliersbook.com.

Click on the Accidental Diminisher Quiz link
to complete the online assessment.

To conduct a complete 360-degree assessment or to
measure how much intelligence you or your team is
accessing from the people around you, contact:

The Wiseman Group at www.TheWisemanGroup.com

or send an e-mail to info@TheWisemanGroup.com.

NOTES

FOREWORD BY STEPHEN R. COVEY

1. Peter F. Drucker, *Management Challenges of the 21st Century* (New York: Harper Business, 1999), 135.

CHAPTER 1: THE MULTIPLIER EFFECT

1. Bono, "The 2009 Time 100: The World's Most Influential People," *Time*, May 11, 2009.
2. Name of leader has been changed.
3. Name of the leader has been changed.
4. Research method and data available in Appendix A.
5. Carol Dweck, *Mindset: The New Psychology of Success* (New York: Random House, 2006).
6. Nicholas D. Kristof, "How to Raise Our I.Q.," *New York Times*, April 16, 2009.
7. Ibid.; Richard E. Nisbett, *Intelligence and How to Get It: Why Schools and Cultures Count* (New York: W.W. Norton & Company, Inc., 2009).
8. Gary Hamel and C.K. Prahalad, *Competing for the Future* (Boston: Harvard Business School Press, 1994), 159.
9. Name of leader has been changed.
10. Carol Dweck, *Mindset: The New Psychology of Success* (New York: Random House, 2006), 6.
11. Ibid., 7.
12. Joel Stein, "George Clooney: The Last Movie Star," *Time*, February 20, 2008.

CHAPTER 2: THE TALENT MAGNET

1. Name of the leader has been changed.
2. Carol Dweck, *Mindset: The New Psychology of Success* (New York: Random House, 2006).
3. Dina Kraft, "Israelis and Palestinians Launch Web Start-Up," *New York Times*, May 29, 2008.
4. Jack and Suzy Welch, "How to Be a Talent Magnet," *Business Week*, September 11, 2006.

CHAPTER 3: THE LIBERATOR

1. Name of leader has been changed.
2. Students scoring either "proficient" or "advanced" levels have increased from 82 to 98 percent. Students scoring "below basic" or "far below basic" levels have decreased from 9 to 2 percent.
3. Peter B. Stark and Jane S. Flaherty, *The Only Negotiating Guide You'll Ever Need* (New York: Random House, 2003).

CHAPTER 4: THE CHALLENGER

1. Bill Vlasic, "Mapping a Global Plan for Car Charging Stations," *New York Times*, February 8, 2009.
2. Ibid.
3. Alan Salzman, "The 2009 Time 100: The World's Most Influential People," *Time*, April 30, 2009.
4. Larry Huston and Nabil Sakkab, "Connect and Develop: Inside Procter & Gamble's New Model for Innovation," *Harvard Business Review*, March 2006.
5. Klaus Kneal, "America's Most Powerful CEOs 40 and Under," Forbes.com, January 14, 2009.
6. Interview with Riz Khan, *One on One*, Al Jazeera, broadcast January 19, 2008.
7. Noel Tichy, *The Leadership Engine* (New York: Harper Business, 1997), 244.

CHAPTER 5: THE DEBATE MAKER

1. Standing in the Rose Garden on Tuesday, April 18, 2006, amid pressure to remove Defense Secretary Donald Rumsfeld from his cabinet position, Mr. Bush described his approach to making decisions. He explained, "Don Rumsfeld is doing a fine job . . . I hear the voices, and I read the front page, and I know the speculation. But I'm the decider, and I decide what is best. And what's best is for Don Rumsfeld to remain as the secretary of defense."
2. Joe Klein, "The Blink Presidency," *Time*, February 20, 2005.
3. Michael R. Gordon, "Troop 'Surge' Took Place Amid Doubt and Debate," *New York Times*, August 30, 2008.
4. David Brooks, "The Analytic Mode," *New York Times*, December 3, 2009
5. Quoted in Adam Bryant, "He Prizes Questions More Than Answers," *New York Times*, October 24, 2009.
6. Ibid.
7. Shared Inquiry is a method of learning developed and taught by the Junior Great Books Foundation.

CHAPTER 6: THE INVESTOR

1. Nic Paget-Clarke, Interview in Ahmedabad, August 31, 2003, *In Motion* magazine.
2. "The Big Picture" was developed by Catalyst Consulting.
3. Based on our research survey on the leadership practices of Multipliers and Diminishers. See Appendix B.

CHAPTER 7: BECOMING A MULTIPLIER

1. John H. Zenger and Joseph Folkman, *The Extraordinary Leader* (New York: McGraw-Hill, 2002) 143–147.
2. Name of leader has been changed.

3. Name of leader has been changed.
4. Name of leader has been changed.
5. Piero Coppola, *Dix-sept ans de musique à Paris: 1922–1939* (Lausanne: F. Rouge et Cie, 1944), 105.
6. Bono, "The 2009 Time 100: The World's Most Influential People," *Time*, May 11, 2009.

APPENDIX A: THE RESEARCH PROCESS

1. James C. Collins, *Good to Great: Why Some Companies Make the Leap—and Others Don't* (New York: Harper Business, 2001) 7.
2. Shane Legg, and Marcus Hutter, *Technical Report: A Collection of Definitions of Intelligence* (Lugano, Switzerland: IDSIA, June 15, 2007).
3. Linda S. Gottfredson, "Mainstream Science on Intelligence: An Editorial with 52 Signatories, History, and Bibliography," *Intelligence*, 24(1):13–23, 1997.

INDEX